About the author

Jonathan Glennie has worked as a policy analyst in several international development charities. He is currently Christian Aid's country representative in Colombia. He has played a key role in campaigns in the United Kingdom and around the world, including the Make Poverty History campaign in 2005.

African Arguments

African Arguments is a series of short books about Africa today. Aimed at the growing number of students and general readers who want to know more about the continent, these books highlight many of the longer-term strategic as well as immediate political issues confronting the African continent. They get to the heart of why Africa is the way it is and how it is changing. The books are scholarly but engaged, substantive as well as topical.

Titles already published

Tim Allen, *Trial Justice: The International Criminal Court and the Lord's Resistance Army*
Alex de Waal, *AIDS and Power: Why There is No Political Crisis – Yet*
Raymond W. Copson, *The United States in Africa: Bush Policy and Beyond*
Chris Alden, *China in Africa*
Tom Porteous, *Britain in Africa*
Julie Flint and Alex de Waal, *Darfur: A New History of a Long War*
Jonathan Glennie, *The Trouble with Aid: Why Less Could be More for Africa*

Forthcoming

Peter Uvin, *Life after Violence: A People's Story of Burundi*
William Gumede, *The Democracy Gap: Africa's Wasted Years*
Camilla Toulmin, *Climate Change in Africa*

Published by Zed Books and the IAI with the support of the following organizations:

InterAfrica Group The InterAfrica Group is the regional centre for dialogue on issues of development, democracy, conflict resolution and humanitarianism in the Horn of Africa. It was founded in 1988 and is based in Addis Ababa, with programmes supporting democracy in Ethiopia and partnership with the African Union and IGAD. <www.sas.upenn.edu/African_Studies/ Hornet/menu_Intr_Afr.html>

International African Institute The International African Institute's principal aim is to promote scholarly understanding of Africa, notably its changing societies, cultures and languages. Founded in 1926 and based in London, it supports a range of seminars and publications including the journal *Africa*. <www.internationalafricaninstitute.org>

Justice Africa Justice Africa initiates and supports African civil society activities in support of peace, justice and democracy in Africa. Founded in 1999, it has a range of activities relating to peace in the Horn of Africa, HIV/AIDS and democracy, and the African Union. <www.justiceafrica.org>

Royal African Society Now more than a hundred years old, the Royal African Society today is Britain's leading organization promoting Africa's cause. Through its journal, *African Affairs*, and by organizing meetings, discussions and other activities, the society strengthens links between Africa and Britain and encourages understanding of Africa and its relations with the rest of the world. <www.royalafricansociety.org>

Social Science Research Council The Social Science Research Council brings much-needed expert knowledge to public issues. Founded in 1923 and based in New York, it brings together researchers, practitioners and policymakers in every continent. <www.ssrc.org>

JONATHAN GLENNIE

The trouble with aid

Why less could mean more for Africa

Zed Books
LONDON | NEW YORK

in association with

International African Institute
Royal African Society
Social Science Research Council

The trouble with aid: Why less could mean more for Africa was first published in association with the International African Institute, the Royal African Society and the Social Science Research Council in 2008 by Zed Books Ltd, 7 Cynthia Street, London N1 9JF, UK and Room 400, 175 Fifth Avenue, New York, NY 10010, USA

www.zedbooks.co.uk
www.internationalafricaninstitute.org
www.royalafricansociety.org
www.ssrc.org

Cover designed by Rogue Four Design
Set in OurType Arnhem and Futura Bold by Ewan Smith, London
index: <ed.emery@thefreeuniversity.net>
Printed and bound in UK by Good News Press, Ongar

Distributed in the USA exclusively by Palgrave Macmillan, a division of St Martin's Press, LLC, 175 Fifth Avenue, New York, NY 10010.

A catalogue record for this book is available from the British Library
Library of Congress Cataloguing in Publication Data available

ISBN 978 1 84813 039 5 hb
ISBN 978 1 84813 040 1 pb

Contents

Acknowledgements

This book has benefited from the input of many friends and colleagues, either directly commenting on the text or during discussions. The initial paper was presented at the UN Economic Commission for Latin America and the Caribbean and thanks are due to the team there, especially to Juan Carlos Moreno, for giving me the opportunity to elaborate the structure of my argument. Thanks to Richard Dowden for suggesting the book, to Robert Molteno for encouraging me to write it, and to David Woodward, Dereje Alemayehu, Alex de Waal, Alex Wilks and Ian Knowles for their very helpful comments. Special thanks to Charles Abugre who has shared with me the insights gained from his many years of service. Finally, thanks to my parents, who taught me most of what I know.

The views expressed in this book are mine and do not necessarily represent the views of Christian Aid or any other organization for which I have worked.

Abbreviations

AFRICOM	United States Africa Command
CPIA	Country Policy and Institutional Assessment
DAC	Development Assistance Committee
DBS	Direct Budget Support
EPI	Expanded Programme on Immunization
FDI	foreign direct investment
GBS	General Budget Support
GDP	gross domestic product
GNI	gross national income
GFATM	Global Fund to Fight AIDS, TB, and Malaria
HIPC	Highly Indebted Poor Country
IFF	International Finance Facility
IMCI	integrated management of childhood illnesses
IMF	International Monetary Fund
MCA	Millennium Challenge Account
MDGs	Millennium Development Goals
NGO	non-governmental organization
ODA	official development assistance
OECD	Organisation for Economic Co-operation and Development
PAF	Performance Assessment Framework
PARPA	Action Plan to Reduce Absolute Poverty (Mozambique)
PEPFAR	US President's Emergency Plan for AIDS Relief
UNCTAD	UN Conference on Trade and Development
UNDP	United Nations Development Programme
USAID	United States Agency for International Development
WTO	World Trade Organization

1 | Time to think again

Africa is poor.* If rich countries send it money it will be less poor, and people living in poverty will be better off. It seems perfectly logical, doesn't it? Millions of people in the rich world, moved by images on television and disgusted by the miserable poverty endured by so many people in other countries, have joined campaigns to persuade their governments to give more aid to Africa and help put an end to such shameful inequality. It is not even much of a sacrifice – by any measure rich countries are incredibly mean with their charity, giving between 0.95 per cent (Norway) and 0.16 per cent (the United States) of their annual incomes to countries much poorer than their own.[1]

The year 2005 saw the biggest campaign for more aid the world has ever seen. The Make Poverty History campaign in Britain, which culminated in a 250,000-person march in Edinburgh for the Gleneagles G8 summit in July, was supported by the ONE campaign in the United States and movements and marches in countries across the globe. At the same time the Live 8 concerts were watched by over a billion people and provided a reminder of the first Live Aid concert twenty years before, perhaps the first time the global public joined together in horror at unnecessary suffering in Africa. The campaigns of 2005 were remarkably successful. Millions of people were mobilized on issues that do not directly affect them, and the key demand – more aid – was fairly well answered by the governments of rich countries. In the United Kingdom, ending poverty in Africa became a serious political issue in an election year, with all the main parties lining up behind the campaign's main demand. First the countries of the European Union, then the G8 group of the world's richest

* Unless otherwise stated, Africa refers to sub-Saharan Africa.

countries, pledged vast increases in their aid giving to Africa, doubling 2005 amounts in a matter of years. In the United States, where aid was already going through an exponential revival in its fortunes, the ONE campaign used the momentum of 2005 to build a supporter base now totalling almost 2.5 million people for its headline demand that the country give at least 1 per cent of its annual government expenditure in aid. All fourteen major presidential hopefuls in the US 2008 election, Republican and Democrat, pledged continued increases in aid to Africa to combat disease and hunger. One, Mike Huckabee, demonstrated a worthy, if naïve, personal commitment by promising 'I will build water and sanitation infrastructure and invest in increasing agricultural productivity.'[2] If only it were that simple. This statement is instructive because it demonstrates the fundamental lack of understanding of the complex political channels through which aid is spent, which characterized all the presidential candidates and many of those who, out of sympathy and a sense of justice, demand more aid.

When I first became involved in the global movement to end poverty, calling for more aid seemed to me to be the most obvious of all the things campaigners could do. More aid equals less poverty. More aid equals more schools and hospitals. More aid equals fewer children dying of preventable diseases. More aid equals more roads and infrastructure to support developing economies. It seems simple. But it isn't. Official aid to Africa (that is, money given by governments or international financial institutions funded by governments, as distinct from private charity giving) has many harmful effects that have actually increased poverty in Africa and put off the development of states capable of fulfilling the rights and needs of African citizens. In reality, in many African countries aid has meant more poverty, more hungry people, worse basic services for poor people and damage to already precarious democratic institutions. Over time, looking at the reality of aid, checking the statistics, and talking with people who see how aid has set back their country's development rather than strengthened it, I have slowly come to accept that aid is not the answer to Africa's poverty. Government-to-government aid will always have an important supporting role to play, a role it has played with occasional success over the years. In some countries in the world, depending on their economic and political contexts, aid increases may be appropriate and helpful. But most countries in Africa, rather than seeking more aid, should be reducing the amount they accept. This book will explain why.

Many of those who fondly remember the euphoria of the Live Aid concerts of 1985 have grown to be seasoned campaigners on development and African issues. And the movement for change has grown up with them. What started as an outpouring of emotion has had to get smart. The contrast between an Irish rock star begging viewers to 'Give us your fucking money'[3] and the highly complex demands of the recent Trade Justice campaign, with its analysis of everything from import tariffs to investment regulation, could hardly be more striking. Nevertheless, while campaigns to help the poor of Africa have certainly diversified, that central logic espoused so inspiringly by Bob Geldof in the mid-1980s has remained constant. There are campaigns on everything from fairer trade to women's rights, primary education to climate change. But when the really major campaigns get going, the main answer to the question 'How can rich countries best help poor countries?' is still, 'Give more'. The difference is that a call for personal donations (the Live Aid concerts raised tens of millions of dollars from individual givers) has developed into a demand that governments give more – and not just millions, but tens of billions of dollars more. And governments of the rich nations have responded. Aid is rising year on year, although the ambitious targets set by donors have not been reached. In the words of the new Secretary General of the Organisation for Economic Co-operation and Development (OECD), 'We are talking here about an increase in official development assistance [ODA, the technical term for official aid] of a magnitude and in a time frame that has never been attempted before in the history of the aid effort.'[4] In percentage terms the global aid increases are more significant in Africa than anywhere else (not counting the vast sums of money currently being spent in the post-war Middle East). Official data show ODA to Africa either doubling or almost tripling since the millennium, depending on which figures you use, with predictions of more increases in the years to come.[5]

But the optimism that a big aid push will make a big difference to the lives of poor Africans is not shared by most analysts on the African continent. While there is broad agreement in the 'international development community' in donor countries that more aid is a good thing (even though there is disagreement about how it should be spent), African commentators, who are aware of the real effects of aid over the last decades, tend to be more ambivalent. There is a range of views on the issue; the debate about how to finance urgent needs in Africa is a complex one. But while most African governments generally work hard to increase the amounts of aid they receive, African civil society, such as non-governmental organizations (NGOs, often charities), labour unions and social movements, is not vocal in calling for more aid. African analysts appear not to believe that huge aid increases are the way to achieve growth and development. Many explicitly reject the idea, and it is hard to find a single example of an African NGO that is actively campaigning for aid increases. In a literature review, Moses Isooba of Uganda's Community Development Resource Network found that, 'A majority of civil society actors in Africa see aid as a fundamental cause of Africa's deepening poverty.' He goes on to acknowledge that aid can make 'a lasting difference in helping people to lift themselves out of poverty', but calls for a radical rethink about the purpose and nature of aid giving.[6] Charles Lwanga-Ntale of Development Research and Training (DRT), a Ugandan NGO, describes what he perceives as 'almost unanimous pessimism among African civil society and academia about the unworkable nature of aid, given the way in which it is structured and delivered'.[7] According to Siapha Kamara of the Social Enterprise Development (SEND) Foundation of West Africa, 'mainstream African civil society, especially the emerging independent grassroots based development agencies, think tanks, research and policy advocacy organizations are justifiably asking what is different in the present day international aid architecture. Official Africa tends to be more enthusiastic about the anticipated increase in international aid than civil society ... the more African governments are dependent on international aid the less ordinary citizens such as farmers, workers, teachers or nurses have a meaningful say in politics and economic policies.'[8]

Why? Why should so many experts in Africa, and not only in Africa but across the world, question the good aid is doing them? Is it sensible to suggest that aid could be 'a fundamental cause of Africa's deepening poverty'? Do a 'majority of civil society actors in Africa' really believe so? And why should receiving more aid mean that ordinary people have less of a 'meaningful say in politics and economic policies'? While most people in rich countries consider aid to be a simple act of generosity, Africans understand its far more complex nature. In this book I look at some of the reasons why so many Africans are against more aid. Aid has many impacts, some obvious, some subtle, some quantifiable, some hard to measure, some not really important, some fundamental. *Direct impacts* are the easiest to measure and are the ones we hear about most in the media – how many people have been vaccinated, how many schools have been built, and so on. But also in this category, and perhaps not publicized quite so much, are the harmful side-effects of aid, such as when people are displaced by large projects like dams and mines. Even more controversial are the *policy conditions* attached to aid, which have arguably had greater consequences in the lives of Africans than the direct consequences of the way the money has actually been spent. Within two decades the whole economic direction of a continent has changed, largely as a consequence of aid, and while some people have gained, many more have suffered as a result. It is generally agreed that shortcomings in the accountability and effectiveness of African governments in recent decades have been a major part of the problem of low or negative growth and insignificant poverty reduction. What is less discussed, but is becoming increasingly clear, is that dependency on aid from foreign donors has undermined the development of the *basic institutions* needed to govern and the vital link of accountability between state and citizen. This has retarded African development in fundamental and long-lasting ways. It is what Kamara was referring to when he talked about ordinary people not having a meaningful say in decisions about how their countries are run. Finally, receiving large amounts of aid also has *macroeconomic consequences* because large inflows of foreign money affect prices and incentives. If they are not managed well these effects can be very damaging to poor people. These issues are discussed in more detail in Chapters 3 to 6 of this book.

Following months of pressure around the globe for more aid the G8 met in Scotland in July 2005 and released a communiqué promising substantially more aid, though not all that was being demanded. One leading UK NGO (Oxfam, but it could have been any) commented that, 'The G8's aid increase could save the lives of five million children by 2010 – but 50 million children's lives will still be lost because the G8 didn't go as far as they should have done. If the $50 billion increase had kicked in immediately, it could have lifted 300 million people out of poverty in the next five years.'[9] This kind of claim is common on the campaigning circuit. Campaigners need to make clear statements about the impacts of policies. But even allowing for the fact that mega-calculations will always be more than slightly arbitrary, but are still important in order to convey something's magnitude, this statement is highly misleading. Why? Because it is made on the basis of a very lopsided analysis, which looks only at the most direct and positive outcomes of aid. If one considers only the positive column in the balance sheet, ignoring all the damaging consequences of aid giving, it is certainly possible that, if spent well, aid money could have the kinds of benefits alluded to. Aid spent well can put children through school, build infrastructure and save lives. But what about all the other impacts? What about those who will lose their livelihoods because of bad policies forced on poor countries by aid conditions? What about the long-term consequences of consistently immature and unaccountable state institutions? What about the possibly harmful effects on exchange rates and prices with the serious consequences they might have on workers and consumers? Where are these impacts taken into account when we calculate millions of lives saved per billions of aid dollars spent? Nevertheless, this kind of simplification is common in all sectors of the aid community. Gordon Brown, British Prime Minister and respected economics heavyweight and champion of ending poverty in Africa, has stated simply: 'Let us double aid to halve poverty,'[10] while the United Nations has for years publicized a similarly neat calculation.

Some who have criticized aid have simply called for it to end. Others have gone even further and argued that there is virtually nothing helpful the West can do for Africa. I don't share either conclusion. Yet I do want to challenge the simplistic notion that more aid equals less poverty, and to suggest a new way of approaching aid. I am going to insist that we look at the evidence. All the evidence. In contrast to aid optimists and aid pessimists, who selectively use evidence either to support or dismiss aid, I emphasize that the impacts of aid are complex, some good, some bad. Only when we assess these impacts dispassionately and systematically can we have any real expectation of making a positive and sustained impact on human rights, development and poverty reduction in Africa. I call this approach aid realism.[11] Aid realism means not getting swept away by the ethical clamour to 'do something' when a proper analysis shows that what is being done is ineffective or harmful. And it means not bowing to an ideological anti-aid position in the face of the rights and urgent needs of millions of people. It means carefully analysing the overall impact of aid on Africa, first to see how it can be improved and second, and more importantly given that improving aid will be a very hard job, questioning aid's importance in relation to other policies and factors that influence development and poverty reduction in Africa.

We should emphatically not conclude that the West should therefore somehow leave Africa alone. The corollary of the argument 'something must be done – give more aid' has often appeared to be 'well if aid doesn't work, nothing can be done'. This is very far from the truth. African civil society, while heavily criticizing aid, is not sitting on its haunches in despair, and nor should anyone else. There are many positive measures that rich countries should take right now in order to help Africans reduce poverty and improve human rights. In fact, it will be almost impossible for African governments to reduce their reliance on aid without the international community taking a range of supporting measures. If the first reason to stop campaigning for aid increases is that aid may be doing more harm than good in some countries, the second is that all the emphasis on aid is obscuring the far more important policies the West should be adopting to help Africans out of poverty. The fact that aid dominates our thinking is one of the reasons that these other, more important, actions are not being taken – rich country leaders are not feeling enough political pressure to make the important changes. Aid is easier, and it benefits donors, never mind all the problems it brings with it. I look at these issues in more depth in the last two chapters of the book.

I know it will be troubling reading for some who share something of my own journey, and for many around the world who have only so recently celebrated the renewed commitment that has been wrung out of Western governments to make aid to Africa a priority. But we need to look at the reality of what aid to Africa can mean and to question the assumptions which have dominated for too long, because unless we do we could end up being complicit in making poverty in Africa even worse and deepening the already vast gap between the world's richest nations and those which are home to the world's most desperately poor. Aid increases may harm efforts to reduce poverty and improve governance and sustainable development in most African countries. Those concerned with development in Africa need now to recognize the evidence and challenge generalized calls for more aid. (These arguments do not relate to private aid giving from charities and NGOs, which has few of the harmful consequences of large-scale official aid, partly because it is relatively small, and partly because it is spent very differently.)

The turning point for me was the Make Poverty History campaign, an unprecedented opportunity to concentrate on what developed countries can do to help end the disgrace of poverty in Africa, undermined by simplistic calls for more aid. In the summer of 2005, when the Live 8 concerts rocked the globe, Bob Geldof was quoted as saying, 'Something must be done; anything must be done, whether it works or not.'[12] Even if we charitably put this down to a slip of the tongue, such an attitude does nothing to help the millions of Africans living in poverty. It does matter if it works or not.

This book has one simple purpose: to persuade those concerned about fighting poverty and injustice in Africa to stop calling for more aid, and to focus their attention on issues that will make a real difference to poor people.

2 | The new aid era

Aid to Africa began in the late 1950s as African countries began to win their independence.[1] Economic growth was slow but encouraging between 1960 and 1980, as new African states sought to establish strong institutions, with per capita income growing by 36 per cent (compared to a fall of 15 per cent between 1980 and 2000).[2] Between 1960 and 1975 nine of the world's fifty best-performing countries were in Africa, including Gabon, the fastest-growing developing country of the period.[3] At this time aid comprised 2.3 per cent of the region's GDP (gross domestic product) – more or less equivalent to its annual income.[4] The World Bank, a development bank set up by the major world powers in the aftermath of the Second World War, quickly grew into its role as the world's main aid giver, while its sister organization, the International Monetary Fund (IMF), which was set up to support countries in serious foreign exchange deficit, took longer to take on what over time has become its decisive role in lending to Africa and influencing its political direction. The African Development Bank was founded in 1964 and has played a supporting role to its bigger siblings in Washington. Meanwhile the OECD launched its Development Assistance Committee (DAC) whose membership, which comprises the world's twenty or so richest countries, is responsible for around 90 per cent of global aid flows.[5]

In the second half of the 1970s post-independence economic growth halted sharply: Africa needed help. Steep rises in the cost of oil coincided with collapsing prices for Africa's main exports. African governments sought urgent external grants and cheap loan financing to cover shortfalls in their access to foreign exchange, hoping that a swift end to the global recession would restore commodity prices. It didn't. From 1980 onwards, aid to Africa has been characterized by ever deepening dependence and the aggressive use of aid conditions to enforce the infamous Washington Consensus, coordinated by the World Bank and IMF. Africa replaced South and Central Asia as the leading recipient of aid, moving from receiving around 21 per cent of global aid (from 1960 to 1980) to up to 35 per cent in this period.[6] Official development assistance to Africa reached a peak in 1990 following a decade of intense structural adjustment lending (so called because the conditions attached to aid were intended to lead to 'structural' changes in recipient economies). Then, in the 1990s, aid began to fall both in real terms and as a percentage of rich countries' GNI. By 1997 it was back to 1983 levels.[7] Most analysts regard the declining need to make payments to Cold War allies as a major reason for this decline, but the failure of 1980s policies to halt growing poverty in Africa, and the increasing number of analyses sceptical of the poverty-reducing impact of aid, were all important factors in the downward pressure on aid budgets.

This downturn is unique in the history of aid to Africa, which has otherwise risen gradually, if unevenly, over the last fifty years. It ended at the turn of the millennium when Africa entered what can be characterized as a new era of aid, both because of the additional quantities of aid being transferred, and also because of the renewed optimism about what it can achieve, contrasting with the pessimism of the 1990s. In 1999 aid to Africa increased for the first time since the 1980s, and donors have continued steadily to increase their aid, with a special focus on Africa and promises of even bigger increases in the future.[8] The UN Millennium Summit in 2000, which set out bold new development targets (the Millennium Development Goals), was a manifestation of this new belief in aid as a vehicle for development in Africa. In this chapter we look at the quantity of money being shifted in this new era of aid, what it is intended to achieve, and, finally, what makes this era unique.

Aid is going up again

Global aid levels have been rising for almost a decade. Debt deals brokered between rich country creditors and Iraq and

Nigeria in 2005 led to a huge spike in ODA (which counts debt relief), which in turn meant that the headline figures for aid actually fell in 2006 for the first time since 1997. But the upward trend is clear. ODA, excluding debt relief, was $25 billion higher in 2007 than it was in 2000 ($15 billion higher in real money when you factor in inflation).[9] But this is still only half the story. As well as the debt deals, global figures have been distorted by the massive increases in post-war aid to Afghanistan and Iraq: they do not tell us what is happening in Africa. When we look at the data by region, we see that while aid overall is rising but undramatically, aid to Africa is experiencing an unprecedented surge. It is a matter of debate whether or not to include debt relief in the aid figures. When a country is paying back its debt, relief is an important boost to the government coffers. This has been the case with most of the African debt cancelled by the World Bank and IMF during the Make Poverty History campaign. But if the debt is not being paid back then cancelling it is more of an accounting exercise than anything else. The Nigerian multi-billion-dollar debt buy-back is a case in point.

Without studying individual country accounts it is hard to know whether to include debt relief, so we shall look at both sets of figures. Excluding debt relief, and taking inflation into account, aid to Africa has increased by 81 per cent since 1999, the year aid started to climb again in Africa. When we ignore the effects of inflation, aid has more than doubled. This is the fastest growth in aid Africa has seen since the end of the 1970s. In 2007 aid to Africa (excluding debt relief) increased by 10 per cent in real terms, even faster than in previous years.[10] When we include debt relief, which has been a major boon for Africa in recent years, the figures are even more impressive, with a near tripling of aid to Africa since 1999 (in part because the Nigeria deal was so big). Predictably, aid rises have not been as fast as promised by rich country leaders in the various pledging rounds that have hit the news, and doubling aid from 2004 levels by 2010, as promised, now looks unlikely. But that should not obscure the fact that aid to Africa will continue to rise in what the DAC has called 'the largest expansion of ODA ... since the committee was formed in 1960'.[11]

Although often derided as mean (it gives the smallest percentage of its income in aid of any OECD country), the United States is the world's biggest donor, accounting for 21 per cent of aid in 2007.[12] It has led the way on aid increases. The Financing for Development conference in Monterrey in 2002 was the first major pledging round of the new aid era, and President George W. Bush promised a 50 per cent increase in US development assistance by 2006.[13] He achieved that level three years early. Bush quadrupled aid to Africa between 2001 and 2006, from $1.4 billion to $5.6 billion a year.[14] In 2007, the United States again increased ODA to Africa by 4.4 per cent in real terms (excluding debt relief) and it seems set to keep the money coming.[15] Meanwhile, the United Kingdom is taking a lead in Europe, although the Nordic countries, the Netherlands and tiny Luxembourg remain the only donors meeting the global target of giving 0.7 per cent of their GNI in aid.[16] In October 2007 the UK Chancellor, Alistair Darling, recommitted his government to doubling aid to Africa from 2004 levels by 2010, and confirmed that the United Kingdom is on track to reach the 0.7 per cent target by 2013.[17] In May 2005 the EU agreed to double aid by 2010, promising to reach the 0.7 per cent target as a bloc for the first time.[18] Japan appears to be the only major donor decreasing its aid.[19] Korea, a new OECD member and relatively new to the field of aid giving, has pledged to raise aid to 0.1 per cent of GNI, around $1 billion, by 2010. It increased its aid by 43 per cent in 2007.[20] The African Development Bank's concessional lending arm has been a beneficiary of aid increases, with donors pledging to raise their contributions by over 50 per cent between 2008 and 2010.[21]

There has also been a big increase in aid to Africa from countries which have not until recently been considered part of the donor community, most significantly China (although China has been providing aid to African countries since the 1950s).[22] A variety of summits and announcements in recent years have left the world in no doubt regarding China's interest in the continent, but somewhat unclear with regard to the details. China appears to prefer to keep the substance of deals secret and does not appear to share OECD's strict insistence on separating out 'aid' from other flows. The clearest details we have of China's intentions were set out by Chinese President Hu Jintao at a summit with African leaders in November 2006. His eight-point plan included pledges to double aid to Africa by 2009, and cancel the debts of the poorest countries. He also offered to build a conference centre for the African Union to use.[23] Six months later at a meeting of the African Development Bank in Shanghai, China said it was going to provide $20 billion to Africa over three years to finance trade and infrastructure.[24] India has been hot on Chinese heels, pledging billions in loans to Africa in 2008.[25]

What's it all for?

Behind the impressive numbers showing large-scale aid increases, a number of influential reports published in the last few years provide the theoretical and evidential basis for the new era of aid. These reports underpin the aid optimism which is now the political consensus in donor countries, and they seek to reverse the tide of literature which began in the 1990s that seriously questions the impact of aid on poverty reduction. The year 2005 was one in which the United Kingdom and much of the rest of the world focused on Africa, and it is no coincidence that that year saw the publication of two of the most influential reports on eradicating poverty in Africa. The report of the UN Millennium Project, directed by globe-trotting economist Jeffrey Sachs, called for aid to all developing countries to rise to $195 billion by 2015 (from about $80 billion at the time).[26] The report of the Africa Commission, chaired by then UK Prime Minister Tony Blair, called for a trebling of aid to Africa, also by 2015.[27]

What did these reports think such aid would achieve? This may appear an obvious question, but it goes to the heart of the contradictions and dilemmas that beset the new era of aid. Aid is a simple word describing an incredibly complex range of financial transactions, from huge disbursements to governments to tiny contributions to local NGOs. There are countless ways to categorize aid; the simplest is to split it up into just two categories: emergency aid and development aid. Emergency aid is short-term assistance to help a country or region out of a crisis. Development aid is intended to support long-term growth and poverty reduction. They are very different.

Emergency aid

In the final months of 2007 torrential rains and floods swept over central Africa, destroying homes and schools and washing away crops and livestock. Some 600,000 people were left homeless, with many more needing emergency help in nineteen separate African countries from Ghana to Kenya. As it so often does, the global community responded swiftly with large amounts of aid which, although some will be used for long-term rebuilding, was mostly intended to provide food, shelter and basic services for those immediately affected by the disaster. This is emergency aid. Drought is another natural disaster (helped in its devastation, like most natural disasters, by human factors) which spurs the world to give aid – Africa is the best-known recipient of disaster relief for famine. In the modern world it has become common for all countries, rich or poor, to respond generously to natural disasters. Even rich countries accept such help. The United States accepted foreign aid when hurricanes and floods hit New Orleans in 2005.

Emergency or humanitarian aid is the fastest-growing type of aid, partly because recorded man-made and natural disasters are on the increase. It is different from development aid, although it can and does contribute to development objectives. Using money to provide for immediate and basic needs in a restricted geographical area is a different challenge from seeking longer-term and sustainable change. It is easier. Not only does aid often work in these circumstances, it is the only possible humane option. There is no point watching pictures of a famine on the TV and setting out a policy to improve famine-prevention systems in coming years. There are, of course, problems with emergency aid.

It is frequently late and insufficient, it is scandalously strongly associated with how much TV coverage a particular disaster is receiving in donor countries and it sometimes has unintended consequences. But emergency aid accounts for only around 10 per cent of all aid flows. The vast majority of aid is not used to respond to time-limited emergencies, but to chronic problems of poverty. This is development aid.

Development aid

Development aid seeks to make a difference in the short, medium and long term, fostering economic growth and reducing poverty. It is spent on improving healthcare, both by providing direct services such as immunization, and by strengthening health systems, a much longer-term and harder challenge than emergency aid. It is spent on schools and teachers' salaries. It is spent on infrastructure to help the private and public sectors do their work more efficiently. It is spent on large development projects such as hydroelectric dams and oil pipelines, which are considered by the investors to be important to the long-term economic prospects of the recipient countries. This is not about responding to emergencies, but about making clear interventions in social and economic areas with the aim of fostering progress. Naturally, there can be blurred lines between the two categories. The AIDS pandemic that has devastated so much of Africa since the 1980s, slashing life expectancy in Botswana, for example, from fifty-six to thirty-five in the space of one decade, is nothing if not an urgent crisis – an emergency.[28] But it is not a time-limited disaster requiring traditional emergency aid. It requires a longer-term, more holistic response. On the other hand, part of the answer to long-term problems like malaria and other diseases are short-term interventions like vaccinations and mass mosquito net distribution. But a sustainable solution must go beyond immediate responses and focus on systems that work for the long term.

It is clear from the statements of rich world development and finance ministers that aid increases in the new era of aid are primarily intended for development and not emergency humanitarian assistance. Proponents of aid increases heavily emphasize longer-term objectives, especially economic growth. Both the major 2005 reports (from the UN Millennium Project and the Africa Commission) emphasize that massive aid increases should form part of a package designed to boost growth in Africa in the short term and for the long term. These two high-profile publications were only the culmination of a rising clamour for hikes in aid since the late 1990s, which led to the UN conference on Financing for Development in Monterrey in 2002 at which rich countries pledged a sea-change in their financial giving to developing countries. The Monterrey Consensus, agreed by all UN member countries, also sees aid as a fundamental part of the long-term development of poor countries. Aid can 'help a country to reach adequate levels of domestic resource mobilization over an appropriate time horizon', it can 'pave the way for robust growth', and it is 'a crucial instrument for supporting education, health, public infrastructure development, agriculture and rural development, and to enhance food security'.[29]

According to the proponents of more aid, the problem is clear: high rates of poverty and low rates of economic growth. The solution: lots of money from donors as part of a package to lead to the sustainable growth of African economies. More aid is necessary, according to the Millennium Project, in order to 'kick start' growth, while the Africa Commission emphasizes the importance of large sums of aid for what it calls a 'big push' for growth. Spurred on by the urgency of the need, which is undisputed, we want to do something now, as when we rapidly build shelters for people made homeless by war or floods. We want to achieve development in a hurry. Some governments, led by the British, are so convinced of the importance of getting aid to Africa as soon as possible in the hope that it will swiftly transform the chances of African economies that they have endorsed the idea of 'frontloading' aid. They are seeking to borrow from private lenders in order to increase their aid giving in the next few years, either with a mind to reducing it after 2015, or in the hope of having found more sustainable sources of aid financing by then. In 2015 they would start repaying what they had borrowed with interest. Even if aid giving were to go down at this point (an issue they are careful to remain ambiguous on) it wouldn't matter, it is implied, because so much will have been achieved through the effective spending of very large amounts of aid in the previous ten years (2005–2015). The elaboration of the UN's internationally agreed Millennium Development Goals (MDGs) have focused aid interventions even more sharply on short-term results. The MDGs are targets on poverty, health, education and other human development indicators with completion dates – most are to be met by 2015.

Development takes time

But at the heart of the humanitarian desire to help and help fast there is a dilemma. Development needs time as well as money. The very word implies progressive steps over time. Historical processes that have over centuries led to strong institutions in developed countries cannot be implanted overnight. This is the difference between emergency aid and development aid. Emergency aid often has to ride rather roughshod over politics and systems in order to reach the people in need. That is sometimes necessary, but it doesn't always help long-term development, and frequently hinders it. When there is famine in Africa the humane response is to fly in large quantities of food – don't think too hard about the politics or economics of it, just save lives. But in order to respond to the *causes* of the famine we do have to think about politics and economic policies, about how farmers can produce more food sustainably in the long term. Food aid can even make the causes of a famine worse, while helping save lives in the short term. The arrival of food aid (especially when late) can have adverse effects on farmers, depressing prices in the area, reducing profitability for food producers and destroying markets, leaving them poorer and less able to pay for food and basic services.

Similar dangers arise with other short-term goals. While it is a useful idea to have targets like the MDGs to coordinate efforts and highlight urgency, focusing on deadlines and targets is a very different equation from emphasizing structures and sustainability. It would theoretically be possible to reach the MDGs without successfully laying the groundwork for long-term development, and vice versa. Helicoptering in food for the hungry every year until 2015 could mean success according to the MDG target on hunger and malnutrition, but would do nothing for food security and could worsen the long-term prospects of hungry people by altering incentives and prices. Equally, setting in trend a sustainable system of healthcare in parts of Africa is likely to take decades. It is quite possible that decisions need to be taken to achieve this that do not sit squarely with the pressure to provide care and medicine rapidly to all. 'Vertical' aid programmes that ship in trained doctors from abroad and set up projects separate from local and quite possibly inefficient health systems might sometimes be the quickest way to get lots of people immunized fast, to get the job done. Initiatives like this have become increasingly popular in this era of aid, and they are not without results. But such an approach can undermine the building of a sustainable health system to serve the population in the years ahead. It can erode public trust in national systems, which takes years to build, and often the best-trained doctors and nurses are poached, leaving national systems weaker than before. On the other hand, the consequences of investing time and effort in transforming a health service that has suffered years of neglect might jeopardize the fast results possible with 'vertical' interventions. With limited amounts of time, money and human resources, what decisions do you make? These are the kind of trade-offs politicians all over the world make every day, short term versus long term. So, although the objectives of swift progress and sustainable development are mentioned in one breath by politicians and proponents of a new era of aid to Africa, in the real world it is important to distinguish between them.

Today's aid is increasingly focused on short-term targets. In the first half of the 1990s the share of aid to Africa being spent on infrastructure (such as transport and energy) and economically productive projects (in sectors such as agriculture, industry and services) was 53 per cent. This kind of spending has a long-term results horizon and may not lead to the sort of quick improvements in human development indicators aspired to in the MDGs. Ten years later (in the period 2000–2004) the proportion of aid spent in these areas had reduced dramatically to only 31 per cent. Meanwhile, spending on social sectors (such as health and education) had risen as a proportion of aid to Africa from 33 per cent to 60 per cent.[30] One of the clearest examples of confusion over the time horizons involved in development interventions is the UN Millennium Project's list of what it calls 'quick wins', interventions that donors can supposedly make right away for Africa, with immediate results. While the suggestions are quite sensible, the idea that somehow they can be successfully implemented so immediately is rather unrealistic – some more than others. The distribution of insecticide-treated bed-nets to all children to cut malaria infections is sensible, and such initiatives in some African countries, including Ethiopia, appear to be producing results.[31] But another supposed quick win verges on the absurd: 'Empower women to play a central role in formulating and monitoring MDG-based poverty reduction strategies and other critical policy reform processes, particularly at the level of local governments.'[32] The empowerment of women and women's rights in general is one of the most complex of all cultural issues around the world. In every different context communities have a different way of approaching an issue which will take many decades to play out. The idea that this could be a 'quick win' is a strange one.

A common exercise among development economists in the last few years has been calculating the so-called 'MDG financing gap' – how much extra money poor countries need to achieve the MDGs given the low level of savings generally available in these countries. If you are faced with an emergency situation the sensible course of action is to send in money and resources fast. But chronic poverty in Africa should not be treated as an emergency. Urgency is important in this business, given the scale of the crises and difficulties facing so many families in Africa, but so is patience. We must be careful that our interventions help not only in the short term but build for the long term. Politics matters. 'Good governance', as it is known in the jargon, is both an end in itself and also perhaps the most important means to achieving growth and poverty reduction. If Africans are going to build economies in which the market thrives, institutions are accountable and the fundamental rights of all are respected, they will need time. We should be cautious about supporting interventions that undermine this long-term ambition, even if they produce valuable short-term results.

From independence to dependency

Because policies and institutions are so important the subject of aid dependency is fundamental to an analysis of aid in Africa. Dependency is the one issue that, more than any other, separates this period from previous periods of aid enthusiasm. Some of the characteristics of the new aid era appear new but are variations on old themes. The War on Terror has replaced the Cold War as the dominant Western security concern, but its implications for the distortion of aid from poverty reduction to bolstering strategic allies are similar. One of the dominant themes of aid has been aid conditions, and they remain key in this era too, although having received a great deal of criticism they are undergoing further metamorphoses. Problems have long been identified with aid giving, and attempts made to rectify them, so the idea that major changes need to be made to the 'aid architecture' is hardly new. But it has become even more central today. The 'Better Aid' agenda, which we will look at in Chapter 7, began formally at the Rome Conference on Aid Harmonization in February 2003. The rhetoric is similar to previous eras, with promises to double aid, to ensure country ownership, to reach a group of internationally agreed targets and, this time, to end poverty for good. To the untrained ear these appear to be signs of hope that aid giving is undergoing a transformation that will make it more effective than before. But more seasoned observers remember similar calls in past aid eras, since the 1950s.[33] Little has changed.

But there is one characteristic that is fundamentally different in this new aid era: short-term aid support has turned into long-term aid dependency. Aid dependency can be measured by looking at aid as a percentage of a recipient country's GDP and seeing how that ratio changes over time. When aid started in the 1960s it accounted for 2.3 per cent of African GDP, similar to the figure for South Asia (home to large aid recipients like India and Bangladesh).[34] But what has happened since is instructive. While aid to South Asia has steadily declined, and now makes up around 1 per cent of GDP, in Africa the trend has gone the other way, skyrocketing in the 1980s and hardly falling since. It now averages around 9 per cent of GDP across Africa.[35] There are wide variations across countries. Some, like Nigeria and South Africa, receive a tiny amount of aid, and a handful of others, like Gabon, have tended to keep levels low, at around 3 per cent or less. But countries receiving less than 10 per cent of their GDP in aid, which is still far more than most countries in the world, are the exception. More typical are Mali (13 per cent), Mauritania (17 per cent), Malawi (20 per cent), up to Sierra Leone and Burundi (over 30 per cent).[36]

Here lies the difference. Since the turn of the century, when this new era of aid began, aid increases have been directed not to countries hoping for a fillip to help them out of short-term trouble, but to countries now severely dependent on aid. When we look at aid levels in the rest of the developing world, the contrast is stark. Only a handful of countries scattered across the globe, such as Nicaragua and Haiti and the small islands of Oceania, come close to this type of aid dependence. India, which in 1960 received levels of aid similar to those now received in Africa, has reduced that level to under 0.2 per cent, a story repeated across South and Central Asia. Vietnam, which has seen aid rise significantly since the 1980s, still relies on it for only 4 per cent of its GDP or less. Poor countries in the Americas have seen aid progressively reduce from 0.7 per cent of GDP in the 1960s to under 0.3 per cent today. It's not that no other country has ever received large amounts of aid before. The key factor is that very high aid receipts have now lasted for decades in Africa and have become the norm. Korea, like some of the Asian Tiger economies, was a big aid recipient in the 1960s, receiving around 6 per cent of its annual spending money in aid. But by the 1970s that figure was under 2 per cent and it continued to decline rapidly. The same happened in North Africa. Contrast this with the story in sub-Saharan Africa. Benin, Burkina Faso, Ghana and Senegal are among those countries that have been relying on aid for around 10 per cent of their GDP for the last thirty years. For Burundi, Rwanda, Zambia and many others that figure is nearer 20 per cent, while Mozambique and Liberia reach 30 per cent. Guinea-Bissau has received an average of 44 per cent of its GDP in aid since 1980. The Korea of Africa is Botswana, which received high levels of aid in the 1960s and 1970s (averaging 17 per cent of GDP) and whose growth rate at that time exceeded those of Hong Kong, Taiwan, Malaysia and Thailand.[37] But unlike almost all other African countries, aid to Botswana has steadily declined over the decades. Today it receives negligible levels of aid, although its economic boom has been brought to a tragic end by the AIDS pandemic.

These ratios are extremely high and the implications for Africa are profound. Never has any group of countries been so dependent on aid for their basic functioning, let alone for development and poverty reduction, for so long. There is a big difference between receiving aid as a welcome support and needing it as a fundamental part of the national budget. Dependency on foreign governments for financial assistance has undermined efforts to develop in Africa and will continue to do so despite the modern (laudable) emphasis on 'good governance' and 'country ownership'. But while Africa's dependence on aid is frequently commented on, it has had virtually no impact on donor policy. Instead, these worrying trends are set to get worse as promised aid increases start to kick in. While the rest of the world appears to be moving on from aid (with some exceptions), Africa is getting more and more aid dependent.

It is strange that the amount of aid considered appropriate by donors is a percentage of donor country income with no relation to Africa's present economic circumstances (0.7 per cent of *donor country* GNI, as recommended by the Pearson Commission in 1969).[38] Surely targets should be set according to demand rather than supply. In this book I argue that rather than setting targets to increase aid, based on how well donor country economies are doing, we should frequently be setting targets to decrease aid, having analysed more profoundly its impact on recipient countries. Some countries, like Botswana, could probably do with more aid again. But others should ideally receive less. Rwanda already pays for half its government spending with aid, not to mention very large amounts of off-budget funding.[39] Rather than seeking to increase this proportion, Rwanda could set itself the goal of reducing it over time. That means that donors would reduce their aid to Rwanda. And other African countries could do the same. Why? Because when looked at overall, when the whole range of aid's impacts are taken into account, it becomes clear that aid at present levels is hindering rather than helping the development prospects of many African countries.

3 | All aid's impacts: the bigger picture

Is aid reducing poverty? Is it contributing to economic growth and strengthening institutions? Now that we have an understanding of the context in which aid is expanding, it is time to explore the substance of the subject. Is it helping poor and marginalized Africans access their rights? Or is it actually increasing poverty and causing economic decline, while harming the development of accountable institutions? Or (more likely) is it doing both? What are its positive and negative effects? Overall, just how important is aid to development in Africa?

Most analyses of the effectiveness of aid can be categorized as belonging to one of two camps: the aid optimists and the aid pessimists. As is demonstrated by the huge aid increases from the beginning of this century, the aid optimists have had the upper hand and have persuaded governments that aid is 'working' and that more aid would work even better. But it was not always so. Until the end of the 1990s the aid pessimists were in the ascendant, as aid fell across the globe and in Africa, with uncertainty about its impact on development. The history of aid analyses has been one of seesawing between these two camps. This is particularly clear in the research studying aid's impact on economic growth; for every study claiming a direct link, another emerges shortly afterwards claiming the opposite. But usually analyses of either type, either optimistic or pessimistic, have tended to be deficient because they have limited their scope to selected impacts of aid rather than its overall impact. The impacts of aid are extremely complex, as I hope to demonstrate in the next few chapters. Different organizations and sectors emphasize different aspects of the aid conundrum. The analyses of this generation of aid optimists tend to avoid discussing some of the negative impacts of aid, despite plenty of evidence, preferring to focus on the success stories. Aid departments write annual reports emphasizing the direct benefits of aid, stating, for example, how $100 million was spent on schools in Cameroon and now 20,000 more children are in education. But they rarely talk about the strings attached to that aid. Campaigners for more aid scour reports to find evidence to support their position, skimming over information that does not. Simplistic notions about 'doubling aid to halve poverty' have been adopted by governments, the UN and civil society alike – but such figures rely on looking only at the positive effects aid can have, and ignoring possible harm.

Some analysts, on the other hand, have put too negative a spin on aid, focusing, for example, on some of the harmful macroeconomic impacts aid can have. Research departments in the IMF produce findings that aid can harm growth because of exchange rate effects, but fail to acknowledge the immediate and important impacts aid can have to save lives and educate people – which is not only a moral imperative but is also likely to be more important to the long-term economy of a country than exchange rates. Some commentators emphasize the self-interest inherent in the actions of aid donors and thus question whether aid is really doing what it claims to be doing. These kinds of critique are helpful and many of the worries are well founded. But highlighting the problems with aid, and some of the less than honourable reasons for aid giving, does not prove that aid cannot be important for poverty reduction. African civil society and a fairly select band of academics appear to be the only sectors that regularly look at the impacts aid has on institutional development. And Western charities are caught in a curious double speak. On the one hand they are some of the most forthright critics of aid conditionality and its harmful effects on Africa. On the other they are the most vocal of all of aid's advocates, emphasizing its direct impacts, and bypassing worrying evidence about its other consequences. Finally, while countless people look at the impact of aid on growth, no one agrees.

What is perhaps surprising is that despite the reams that have been written on aid, and the host of people working in the industry, no holistic analysis attempting to look at *all* its impacts is available. Few even claim to look at aid holistically, and none has done so convincingly. Without such an analysis it is hard to make a judgement about whether aid has helped in the past, and whether it is likely to in the future. The next few chapters take some steps towards addressing this. *All* the various impacts of aid are set out and mapped into an understandable framework. Some of the impacts of aid are intentional, others are unintentional by-products. Some are directly linked to poverty, others less so. I propose four categories to help make an analysis of the 'net' impact of aid on Africa manageable:

1 Direct impacts (this chapter)
2 Policy impacts (Chapter 4)
3 Institutional impacts (Chapter 5)
4 Macroeconomic impacts (Chapter 6)

Only when all these impacts of aid are looked at together can we get a true picture of how aid is affecting development in a recipient country. These categories are to some extent porous, and there will inevitably be overlap. Other analysts will group impacts under different headings or maybe suggest themes not covered even by this attempt to be comprehensive.

It is important to reiterate that we are not dealing here with aid from charities and non-governmental organizations, a topic which could take up an entire book of its own. Although private giving has huge impacts in the areas where it is focused, and although it is on the increase, it is small compared with official aid and remains relatively insignificant compared with the major aid interventions we will be looking at in the following chapters. Some of the issues discussed here will also be relevant to NGO aid, and it has to be said that, along with all the good they do, NGOs also come in for their fair share of criticism. But our focus is on the role played by Western governments in Africa through official (bilateral and multilateral) aid.

Direct impacts

Let us look first at aid's direct impacts. When aid donors look at whether their aid is 'working', especially when they want to justify aid giving to a sometimes sceptical public, they generally look at one thing: the direct impacts of aid (occasionally also calling up the latest economic model linking aid to economic growth). Direct impacts are the most commonly analysed impacts, partly because they are the easiest to evaluate, and partly because they are the elements the aid industry most wants to share with everyone else. The procedure is to take the stated intention of an aid intervention at face value and seek to verify it against what is actually achieved, for instance, x number of children educated, y number of roads built. There is plenty of evidence to show that well-spent aid has helped people in urgent need. The direct, life-saving, impacts of aid are most apparent in emergency situations. When natural disasters strike, foreign governments often play a leading role in providing both money and expertise to ease the suffering of those affected and help them to start again. While, as we have seen, only a small proportion of aid (around 10 per cent) is described as 'emergency' or 'humanitarian', the reality is that many people in Africa live in states of chronic emergency, where basic needs are persistently unmet and urgent help is constantly required.

Evidence for successful aid is particularly strong in targeted programmes with defined objectives, where consistent and sufficient funds have been made available. It is in the field of healthcare that foreign aid's most dramatic successes have occurred, and immunization is perhaps the best example of all. When the Expanded Programme on Immunization (EPI) was launched in 1974 only 5 per cent of children were vaccinated against six key diseases (including diphtheria and tetanus). By 1990 some 75 per cent of children were covered, roughly the same number as are covered today. It is estimated that these vaccinations save about 3 million lives a year, and prevent 750,000 children from becoming permanently disabled.[1] It is clear that vaccinations are among the most cost-effective health interventions available.

It only cost about $100 million to eradicate smallpox the world over (achieved in 1977), while 60,000 cases of river blindness were prevented between 1974 and 2002 at the cost of only $1 per person.[2] These very significant achievements have been paid for in large part with aid money, often bypassing government health systems and going directly to people who most need urgent help. Medicines, especially AIDS drugs, are routinely paid for with aid money, although their availability is still very limited in Africa. By 2005 the Global Fund to Fight AIDS, TB and Malaria (GFATM), founded in 2001, had made grants to 127 countries to put 1.6 million people on anti-retroviral treatment for HIV, provide counselling and testing services, and support children affected by AIDS.[3] According to the OECD, deaths from measles in Africa have fallen by 91 per cent since 2000, thanks to well-focused aid.[4]

Sweeping gains have been made in health and education when aid money (including from debt relief) has been used to replace failing 'cost recovery' programmes that charged poor people to access basic services. Services have to be paid for somehow and, with very small budgets available, many African governments, under pressure from the World Bank and other donors, opted for asking users to pay up-front. The disastrous impact of such policies became evident in Burundi in 2005 when, on the first day of school since the abolition of these 'user fees', an extra 300,000 children turned up to study.[5] Three years earlier, when the government of Tanzania made primary education free and compulsory, an extra 1.6 million children started attending school.[6] Governments in other countries, especially Highly Indebted Poor Countries (HIPC) like Uganda, Zambia and Malawi, that have received substantial debt relief, but also in Kenya which is not an HIPC, now provide schooling free of charge to millions more children.[7] Four million more children have started school in Ethiopia since charges were scrapped.[8] Meanwhile, in the field of health, Uganda has seen a huge increase in attendance at health clinics since user fees were scrapped. Immunization rates have doubled.[9] Many other African countries, like Zambia, have also scrapped user fees for healthcare.[10] Mozambique is using aid money to pay for free immunization for all children, while in Benin, more than half HIPC debt relief has been used to recruit staff for rural health clinics, to promote anti-malaria, HIV/AIDS and immunization programmes, and to improve access to safe water.[11] In all these cases public money is being spent on public services, with significant results. Because of the chronic shortages in the public purse in these countries, aid has been an important source of cash. In that sense aid has worked. Of course, getting policies right has played a more important part. For years the World Bank insisted on user fees for basic services and only recently, under pressure from NGOs, changed its mind.

In some countries infrastructure has also improved. Roads where there was none before have opened up economic opportunities and facilitated the access of basic services. Chad, a country more than twice the size of France, boasts only a few hundred miles of paved roads, making economic growth hard to achieve.[12] Between 1997 and 2005 foreign aid financed around 40 per cent of Ethiopia's road building and improvement programme.[13] Post-conflict assistance has often borne fruit as well, with one of the best examples being the role of the international community, in both military and financial terms, in Sierra Leone. In Mozambique aid reached a very high percentage of government spending once the civil war ended and supported processes of national reconciliation, repatriation of refugees, reintegration of former soldiers and clearing land mines.

There are more examples of the positive direct impacts of aid all readily available in the many reports seeking to pressure for aid increases. In the instances above, and in others, aid has filled a resource gap in the context of very tight African government budgets. We will put these and other similar examples on the positive side of the ledger in our assessment of aid's impacts – financial support for initiatives that meet an important demand. Not surprisingly, when official donors analyse the direct impacts of their aid they find that it is doing rather well. In his book *The Reality of Aid* Roger Riddell has produced the most comprehensive analysis to date of the direct impacts of aid. He looks at a huge number of official reports and finds that in the majority donors have been happy that their aid projects have achieved what they set out to do. Thus the UK, US and Australian development agencies assess that around 75–84 per cent of their projects were successful in 2004, with multilateral agencies recording similar success rates.[14] This said, not all analyses reveal the same good news. According to the World Bank's 1999 Annual Review of Development Effectiveness, to take one example, just 29 per cent of Bank-financed projects in Africa in the 1990s were considered likely to benefit a country's development in the long run.[15] In any case, looking at a development agency's own reporting of its success is a limited methodology. There are strong incentives to emphasize positive outcomes (which makes it even worse when even your own analyses demonstrate failure). To take an example from Latin America, in a 2006 survey on aid effectiveness, donors claimed that nearly a third of their technical assistance was coordinated and aligned to the Nicaraguan government's needs (already a surprisingly small amount). But in the view of the Nicaraguan government itself, 'no current programmes in Nicaragua would qualify as co-ordinated under government leadership'.[16]

In 2006 a group of public health experts from the University of Ottawa charged the World Bank with using ineffective treatments in its malaria programme, and with overstating the effectiveness of the programme by publishing false statistics.[17] Criticisms are normal in any field of public enterprise – one cannot expect an institution as large as the World Bank, or a business as large as the aid business, to be without critics. But it is important to underline something that is already well known, however obvious: aid interventions go wrong as well as right. That has to be taken into account when we assess the overall impact aid has had.

But an even bigger problem is that when government development agencies analyse how their aid is doing they tend not to allow for the possibility that it might have caused harm. Although they invariably find plenty of examples of ineffective aid, they still find that aid is doing some good, although not as much as it could be doing. The reality is, though, that just as there are many examples of aid supporting initiatives that have done a lot of good, there are also many examples where interventions supported by aid money have not only not done much good, but have actively harmed the welfare of some of Africa's poorest people. Sometimes what can by some be considered a great development success is considered by others to be a social, environmental or economic disaster. Controversial aid projects are often ones that focus not on bringing social benefits to people directly, but on boosting the economy – dams that provide energy but lead to mass displacement; roads that help some economic sectors but cut through virgin forest; concessional loans to support large-scale mines or other industries. Let us take one recent example, the Chad–Cameroon pipeline. Costing $3.5 billion and involving a consortium of some of the world's biggest oil companies, the pipeline takes Chad's oil to the coast. World Bank aid was crucial to finalizing the deal. Although only 5 per cent of the total investment (about $175 million), the seal of approval from the Bank was the key to the project getting the go-ahead.[18] Civil society campaigners inside and outside Chad campaigned strongly against the project. In their analysis this was aid doing harm, not good. The pipeline would displace people (numbers depend on whose figures you believe) and carve up national parks (damage depends on whose figures you believe). Crucially, the Chadian government was not considered by many to be an honest broker, with its history of human rights abuses, locking up opposition leaders and embezzling funds. Would the money made by the project, which according to the World Bank would total 50 per cent of the government's revenues, really make it to the poor who needed it most?[19]

When the project was finally passed in June 2000 the World Bank's spokesman summed up the official view as follows: 'No one can guarantee that 100 per cent of the oil revenues will be used responsibly, but one thing is certain: if the oil fields are not developed not a single penny will go to reducing poverty.'[20] Like so many advocates for big aid, he falls into the trap of thinking that, while the intervention may not be perfect, it will at least do some good. What he has not allowed for is the possibility that it could do more harm than good. Did the pipeline actually help or harm Chad's poor? All sorts of measures were taken to try to ensure revenues were spent well, and there is little doubt that the involvement of the World Bank meant the project was less harmful than it otherwise might have been – the World Bank is a public agency spending taxpayers' money and responds to public pressure more than the Chadian government or oil firms might be expected to. But in 2005, two years after the pipeline opened, the World Bank itself joined civil society critics in expressing concern that money was not reaching poor people.[21] Supporters of the project claimed Chadian revenues had increased. But instead of spending the money on health and education, and while civil servants remained unpaid, President Idriss Deby scrapped the revenue management arrangement and used the funds to build up his army.[22] Amnesty International severely criticized the project for the impact it had had on governance issues in Chad.[23] Have the impacts of the pipeline just not been as good as they might have been? Or has the pipeline actively harmed the Chadian people and encouraged bad governance? As fighting erupted in early 2008, many were openly wondering whether this aid-suppported project had brought the oil curse of instability and conflict to another African country.[24]

There are countless other examples of aid projects whose benefits are disputed. The Bujagali hydroelectric dam in Uganda is set to receive support of around $750 million from donors, including the World Bank, the European Investment Bank and the African Development Bank. It will be one of the largest ever investments in East Africa. But Ugandan and international civil society groups have expressed concerns about the impact of the dam on the already declining water levels in Lake Victoria and the harmful impacts on local communities, where thousands of people's livelihoods will be affected (most live from fishing and agriculture) and many will have to be resettled. Meanwhile, even if the project does succeed, only the 5 per cent of Ugandans accessing electricity from the national grid will benefit.[25] What about the $275 million Lower Kihansi Dam which has affected 20,000 villagers in Tanzania? Or the $500 million Manantali Dam in the Senegal River Valley which displaced 12,000 people without full compensation and harmed the livelihoods of around 100,000 more who fish and work on and near the river?[26] These projects are being sponsored by aid from Western donors, and others are receiving aid from China, now a massive investor in these kinds of project in Africa.[27]

It is not obvious that the decisions being made by donors and African governments when they invest in these megaprojects are the wrong ones. The pros and cons all governments have to weigh up when seeking development and progress are complicated, and there are usually losers as well as winners. But there is a reason we hear so little about these kinds of projects in the high-profile publicity about how much good aid is doing in Africa: such projects are controversial, and the impacts are by no means certain to be positive. Millions of dollars of aid money could be supporting widespread human rights abuses and environmental degradation without clear benefits for the poorest and most marginalized. Activist groups in Africa and the West are old hands at campaigning against aid interventions which they see as harmful or dangerous. But while this has led to a certain level of maturity in much of African civil society, which openly discusses the complexities of aid spending and weighs the pros and cons of aid carefully in the balance, in the West aid groups tend to mentally compartmentalize bad aid as separate from calls for more aid. Aid is doing good, and could do even better, they say, rather than accepting that sometimes the opposite is true.

Looking only at the most direct impacts of aid we have seen that while much aid causes some unqualifiedly good things to happen, some aid also supports more controversial projects. It is not just a case of 'could do better', but of causing actual damage. When governments and international NGOs publish reports singing the praises of aid they are not wrong, just unbalanced. It doesn't suit them to look at the down side, so they give it a miss. What we think of aid's impacts is vital to what we think about the possibility of more aid. If we consider that aid, while it could be improved, is basically doing good, we ought to wholeheartedly support major increases in aid. An overall increase in aid would certainly lead to an increase in well-spent aid, on this analysis, even if badly-spent aid also increased. But, as we have seen, the correlation is not so simple. And the bad news, unfortunately, is that we have only just started. We have only surveyed one set of aid's impacts, the direct impacts, which may turn out to be the most positive impacts of all. If we took into account only these we might plausibly conclude that, on balance, the risks that some aid will do harm are outweighed by the opportunities provided by aid to do good. We have to take risks in this business, or we just sit around and moan. But aid's advocates rely too heavily on analyses of the direct impacts of aid, as if these occurred in a bubble, while the many other impacts are often ignored.

4 | Pulling the strings: the reality of aid conditionality

For Africa, like other aid-recipient continents, there have always been two sides to the aid coin. On the one hand, say the donors, we will give you money, but on the other, you have to make some important changes in the way you run your country. Western governments and institutions have got very involved in setting the policy agendas of the majority of countries in Africa over the last twenty-five years and the aid system has been their tool of choice, with trade agreements and other forms of diplomatic pressure used to underpin it. This is particularly true for the most aid-dependent countries. However much people talk about 'ownership', countries agree to conditions only because they have to, and those that depend less on aid find it easier to say 'No'. Aid conditions have gone much further than simple fiduciary and accountability requirements to ensure money is spent as intended. Since the 1980s in particular, when new forms of intrusive conditions became the norm, these 'conditionalities' (as they are technically known) have reached to the very heart of policymaking in Africa, from stipulating how to deliver basic services like health and education to deciding economic policies governing trade and the supply of money to the economy. It is not an exaggeration to say, and many African politicians have done so, that donors led by the IMF and the World Bank have effectively decided key recipient government policies for decades. We have looked at the direct impacts of aid. In this chapter we examine the way aid has been used to overhaul the economic and social policies adopted by governments in Africa. I argue that these impacts on policy are more substantial and longer-lasting and, ultimately, have had greater consequences for poor and marginalized Africans than the direct impacts of aid.

Imposing ideology

It is hard to work in counterfactuals (that is, what African governments would have done had they not had to comply with donor conditionalities), but the balance of evidence suggests that the lasting impact of policy conditions is greater than that of the actual financial resource transfers associated with them. That is certainly what those setting the conditions had in mind. Since the IMF introduced aid conditionality in the mid-1950s, and especially since the concept was formalized with the start of structural adjustment lending by the World Bank in 1979, aid money has had the dual purpose of making direct impacts with the way it is spent and pressuring countries to make sweeping policy reforms that will have lasting consequences for decades to come. The IMF's official justification for its interference in sovereign government policy is that it has a duty to its shareholders to ensure that borrowers make the tough decisions needed to get their economies in a good enough shape to make adequate repayment on IMF loans.[1] Meanwhile, the World Bank had become frustrated supporting countries whose policies it thought would fail – it wanted to restructure economies to produce longer-term effects than project aid could bring about, to make a lasting difference. (Of course, the political masters behind both institutions, rich Western countries, also have their own best interests in mind as they lay down the law in Africa.)

As has often been pointed out, many recipient countries appear to have little to show in terms of poverty reduction from the billions of dollars invested in them by donors. But looking at African policy choices and economic structures today, compared with those at the start of the 1980s, it is clear that most African economies have changed very significantly along the lines of the so-called 'Washington Consensus'.[2] If the aim of aid has been to produce wholesale shifts in the economic policies of recipient countries, then aid has worked. The Washington Consensus describes a set of policies elaborated in the 1980s which the IMF, World Bank and US Treasury Department (all based in Washington) agreed were necessary for poor countries to develop successfully. Joseph Stiglitz, a former chief economist at the World Bank, said in 2004 that, 'If there is consensus today about what strategies are likely to help the development of the poorest countries it is this: there is no consensus except that the Washington Consensus did not provide the answer.'[13] Not so in the heady days of the 1980s and 1990s. IMF and World Bank negotiators were then very clear what African countries needed to do to develop.

The 'Ten Commandments' of the Washington Consensus

1 Tightening government spending across the board
2 Redirecting public expenditure to support growth and pro-poor services
3 Tax reform (lower marginal rates and a broader tax base)
4 Market-determined interest rates
5 Competitive exchange rates to induce growth in exports
6 Reducing barriers to trade
7 Reducing government controls over foreign investment
8 Privatizing state-owned companies
9 Reducing regulations restricting competition
10 Legally enforcing property rights

In theory, not all the policies that made up the Washington Consensus were harmful or even controversial. In many instances, countries were urged to protect property rights, redirect public spending to social services and follow basic laws of fiscal discipline. But in practice even these tenets were applied so rigorously and without regard for political context that they often generated negative outcomes. And those were the good elements. The other policies being forced on African countries are highly controversial and may be doing irreparable damage to a generation of Africans.

Rolling back the state

Primary among these has been trade liberalization, which means for the most part reducing and eliminating import and export tariffs and quotas. Tariffs are taxes used by governments to protect domestic industries from competition and, especially in Africa, have been an important means of raising state revenue. Reducing tariff and quota barriers is a tool available to governments for opening up domestic industries to more foreign competition. Raising such barriers can be equally important, depending on the global and national context, and is exactly what most now-developed countries did when they thought it necessary.[4] But in Africa wholesale tariff reduction was a condition of receiving aid. The landscape of Africa has changed drastically.

When the Kenyan government, under instruction from the IMF, reduced restrictions on imported clothing and deregulated the cotton market, cheap clothing from Asia and Europe flooded into the country, benefiting some consumers in the short term but devastating one of Kenya's most established industries.[5] In 1984, Kenya produced 70,000 bales of cotton per year. By 1995, production had dropped to 20,000. About 320,000 people were directly employed in the industry at the end of the 1980s, a figure which had reduced to 220,000 ten years later. Meanwhile, US subsidies enabled American cotton to be exported at up to 40 per cent less than it cost to produce. By the end of the 1990s, cotton production in Kenya was worth less than 5 per cent of its value in the 1980s. Falling world prices over this period didn't help either. World cotton prices fell by 50 per cent between the mid-1990s and early 2000s, largely due to US domestic subsidies and competitive export promotion in the developing world, destroying poor farmers' livelihoods and generating an estimated foreign exchange earnings loss of $300 million per year in Africa.[6] These policy decisions have long-term effects. In 2001, the United States finally promised African exports duty-free access to the lucrative American market (in exchange for African countries committing to further reform, of course, and without cutting US cotton subsidies).[7] But it was too late. Access was no longer the problem for Kenya's cotton, production was. After years of underinvestment and premature exposure to volatile and distorted global markets, the decades-old Kenyan cotton industry has been unable to resurrect itself. The damage inflicted by aid conditions has long outlasted the aid itself.[8] Tens of thousands of people have been put out of work, and possibilities for generations of future workers dashed. Why? Because of aid.

Tariff reduction has led not only to the devastation of important industries, leading to unemployment and hardship, but has directly affected the size of national budgets and therefore the money available to spend on development. Import tariffs are administratively one of the easiest taxes to impose, a critical point in the African context where state capacity is limited, and they are broadly 'progressive' (that is, they do not hit the poor harder than the rich). In developing countries, especially in the poorest ones, they have contributed significantly to the overall tax take, the most extreme case being Benin which still relies on them for 50 per cent of its tax revenue.[9] An IMF study suggests that while middle-income countries have been able to recover only 45–65 per cent of what they lost in trade tax revenue from other revenue streams, the poorest countries, mostly in Africa, have been unable to find alternatives – they have simply lost the money.[10] So, while on the one hand aid has gone into government coffers, on the other aid has forced countries to dramatically restrict one of their main sources of revenue. And as we shall see in the following chapter, the quantity of money is not the only thing that matters for development; it is also crucial where the money comes from.

Since the IMF and World Bank started using aid conditions to restructure African economies the process has gone through various stages, starting with a focus on cutting budget deficits and inflation and then moving to trade and agricultural liberalization. Trade liberalization conditions are now fewer than in the past, reflecting the extent to which African countries have been corralled into line on the issue. The persistent pressure has shifted towards the privatization of Africa's state-owned enterprises. Privatization works sometimes, if the conditions are right. Too often in Africa the social impacts have been devastating and the outcome little more than the selling off of some of Africa's main sources of government revenue, with inevitable consequences for the state's ability to invest in social services and infrastructure.

Copper exports generate three-quarters of Zambia's foreign exchange earnings and copper prices have skyrocketed since 2003 due to increases in demand, especially from China.[11] You would expect, then, that Zambia is finally making bagfuls of cash from its main industry. It isn't. In the early 1990s the IFIs became fixated on removing mining from state ownership. Aid conditions mandating feasibility studies, and then the sale of mines, were in almost every IFI credit from 1991 onwards. In 1999 major donors withheld $530 million in aid from a Zambian government still reluctant to privatize. The final straw/carrot/stick came when donors made it clear that there would be no relief for Zambia's crippling debt burden without privatization. According to the then finance minister Edith Nawakwi, the IMF and World Bank told Zambia that, 'For the next 20 years, Zambian copper would not make a profit. [Conversely, if we privatized] we would be able to access debt relief, and this was a huge carrot in front of us – like waving medicine in front of a dying woman. We had no option.'[12] The state mining company was split into seven sections and sold to various investors.[13] Since privatization there has been an increase in investment in the industry, with about $1.4 billion being spent on refurbishment and purchases since 1998, and this has meant that the industry is better equipped to make profits from the hike in prices. But the costs have been severe. Jobs in the industry have fallen from around 56,500 in 1991 to under 20,000 in 2004 due to rapid cuts after privatization, and little more than half of the remaining mine workers now have permanent contracts with the associated benefits – the rest are employed by contracting firms.[14] Vitally, profits from the mines are no longer being reinvested in Zambia, but are taken abroad by the foreign owners.[15] And because of the concessions made to foreign companies in order to attract their investment, the government makes next to nothing in tax. The 2005 mining tax take of only $75 million was less than one-third of the contribution made to the national treasury by the state-owned mining company in 1991, even though global copper prices had doubled in the previous two years.[16] In 2006, First Quantum, a Canadian mining company still well within the period of its agreed tax holiday, was so embarrassed that it voluntarily started to pay tax, contributing $19 million to the Zambian government.[17]

Another common conditionality, to complement reductions in import tariffs, has been the reduction in state subsidies to important economic sectors. Groundnuts are the main source of income for more than two-thirds of Senegal's rural population.[18] The industry has for decades received government support through, for example, cheap credit and guaranteed prices. In 2001 the government privatized the collection and sale of the groundnut harvest and the distribution of groundnut seed as part of the conditions it had to fulfil in order to receive IFI funds. According to the Senegalese president, Abdoulaye Wade, 'Against our will we have privatized Sonagraine [the name of the state-run company]. We were forced to do it.'[19] The new private agent-led marketing system led to huge losses for thousands of farmers who received far less for their crops. The resulting poverty led to widespread hunger and children being sent home from school because their families could not afford the fees.[20] In 2005, in response to further IMF and World Bank conditions, Sonacos, the state-run groundnut processing factory, was also privatized.[21]

Undermining basic service provision

Aid donors have also used the power of their money to force African countries to follow IMF-approved public spending regimes which are far stricter than is necessary or prudent. Government spending on education fell by 65 per cent in Africa between 1980 and 1987.[22] The IMF insists that countries it is lending to stay within tight public spending boundaries because of worries about inflation and simply for reasons of good-housekeeping – you shouldn't spend what you don't have. Governments are thus prevented from spending their revenues as they choose, not to mention the aid that sometimes piles up waiting for the IMF go-ahead to be spent. In a survey carried out in 2003, twenty countries were found to have been set targets to achieve fiscal surpluses, thereby restraining public expenditure, at the same time as plans to reduce infant mortality remained under-financed.[23] According to the Global Campaign for Education, wage ceilings set by the IMF in Zambia have meant that teachers were paid the same in 2006 as in 1975.[24] A grant to Uganda from the GFATM was seriously delayed because of IMF concerns over whether it broke tight fiscal boundaries.[25] All this despite evidence suggesting that the threshold at which the negative effects of inflation kick in could be as high as 20 to 25 per cent[26] (the IMF insists on single digits[27]) and reasonably regular reports from within the IMF itself, beginning in the 1990s, criticizing inflation targets for being too low to allow adequate social sector spending.[28]

One of the most damaging of all World Bank strategies in the 1980s and 1990s was the insistence that health and education should not be free at the point of use. Instead, user fees were introduced, with devastating effects on the poor. Whether supporting increased spending on health and education or restricting it through 'fiscal tightening', donors were enforcing policies that prevented poor people accessing these services. By 1995, twenty-eight of thirty-seven countries in Africa had introduced fees for basic healthcare, but in 1998 some 75 per cent of World Bank loans to Africa still included the establishment or expansion of user fees.[29] User fees in Kenya, Zambia, Madagascar, Tanzania and Senegal, among other African countries, led to a decline in the use of maternity and other health services in the poorest communities, contributing to a rise in infant deaths and putting women's health at risk.[30] In Tanzania, the combination of travel costs and user fees in one clinic meant that poor mothers did not bring their children to a doctor until they were very ill, meaning that 53 per cent of children died within forty-eight hours of being seen. The very poorest did not come at all.[31] In Zimbabwe, use of health facilities fell by 25 per cent in three years following the introduction of user fees, while child mortality rose by 13 per cent.[32] The effect was similar in Ghana, Zaire (as it was then called), Swaziland, and Lesotho.[33]

In education the evidence is equally clear. In Kenya, Uganda and Zambia the withdrawal of children from school was a common response to increased costs or reduced household income.[34] When Malawi abolished primary school fees in 1994, enrolment increased by 68 per cent and in Uganda enrolment doubled in 1997 when primary school was made free for four children per family.[35] While fees for schooling are now out of fashion, it is still common to charge for basic healthcare in most African countries. There are some studies, heavily relied upon by the World Bank before it performed its U-turn on user fees, which show take-up of services actually increasing among poor people when user fees are introduced. But the majority show the opposite. According to a UK government report in 2001, 'In virtually all cases where user fees were increased or introduced there has been a concurrent decrease in service utilization. The magnitude of this drop in utilization is frequently larger, and the effect of a longer duration, amongst the poor part of the population.'[36]

Don't blame us!

There are still those who defend economic conditionalities and believe that using aid to pressure countries to liberalize is the right thing to do. According to Paul Collier, former Head of Research at the World Bank, 'the costs of adjustment are largely mythical. Most reforms, if they are sensible, lead to a rapid improvement in the economy.'[37] But these voices are sounding more and more isolated and defensive. The UN Conference on Trade and Development (UNCTAD) describes macroeconomic stability as 'probably the only notable achievement of [structural adjustment]' – by 2004, only three of Africa's fifty-two countries had inflation rates higher than 20 per cent.[38] Some argue that if the Washington Consensus policy framework had been better implemented in Africa, things would have been different. This is the argument of true believers throughout history. 'It's not that communism failed in the Soviet Union, it's that it wasn't followed through with sufficient conviction.' No. It failed because it was economically unsound and politically unviable. So also was the neoliberal experiment in Africa. In the words of Malawi's commerce and industry minister, Sam Mpasu, 'We have opened our economy. That's why we are flat on our back.'[39] It is both amusing and annoying in equal measure when one reads in donor policy papers statements like, 'In recent years, the concept of a "one-size-fits-all" approach has been called into question,' as if suddenly people are discovering all sorts of interesting and previously unknown information.[40] In fact, African governments and civil society organizations have been demanding more policy freedom for decades – it is only in donor circles that the realization is 'recent'.

Some have argued that aid conditions are not to blame for the wholesale shift in direction of Africa's economic and social policies, that African governments must take responsibility for the decisions, and that it has in fact proved impossible for donors to force countries to adopt policies they oppose.[41] This has actually become the orthodoxy in recent years, with leading commentators arguing that unless a recipient government really wants to implement the reforms called for by donors, it is unlikely to do so. There is an element of truth in this argument. African governments have occasionally fought off pressure from donors to implement reforms they oppose. The Mozambican government used the full range of delaying tactics and mustered all its political strength to resist donor pressure on land reform and governance (corruption), the first from a principled position, the second for reasons of transparent self-interest.[42] Strong leadership and contextual factors meant a victory for the Malian government over a World Bank-backed decentralization programme in 2006.[43] The Kenyan government reversed the liberalization of maize marketing, a World Bank condition, no fewer than three times in the 1990s.[44] However, most of the stories in Mozambique, Mali and Kenya, as in most other aid-dependent African countries, have been of subservience to donor requirements, with only occasional resistance. Resistance has tended to delay rather than overturn donor demands, while very limited policymaking and implementing capacity is absorbed, fulfilling (or resisting) donor requirements.

This is clear from a survey of policies typical in Africa after decades of structural adjustment programmes, as well as from a wealth of case-study evidence such as the brief examples above. When we compare today's tariff and subsidy levels with those of twenty-five years ago, when we look at all the privatizations carried out in the 1990s, when we note the homogeneity of the laws governing mining and other foreign investments, when we look at the consistency in the use or non-use of user fees for social services depending on what current World Bank policy happens to be, and on the whole gamut of economic issues, it becomes clear that, under intense pressure from donors, the entire direction of the continent has changed since the early 1980s. A priori, for such a large and diverse group of countries, one would expect a range of responses to the various problems of poverty and development. Instead the response has fitted very much the blueprint designed in Washington. That is no coincidence.

Reform or rehash?

Because of years of campaigning by pressure groups, and a change of heart by some leading donor economists, the reform of aid conditionality is high on the agenda of multilateral institutions and donor governments. Campaigners are constantly told that things are improving or are just about to. Ironically, there are now donor-led processes attempting to increase the ownership of African governments over their economic policy choices. One of the most significant examples is the PRSP (Poverty Reduction Strategy Paper) approach, started with a fanfare at the end of the 1990s, which tries to involve the various sectors of society, along with the government, in drawing up proposals which donors, according to the theory, will then support.[45] Many donors, and some NGOs, saw this as an important step towards country ownership of aid conditions. But was it?

There have been some positive experiences with the PRSP approach. In Ghana it is generally agreed that civil society successfully influenced the PRSP towards a focus on the especially poor areas of the country, while in Zambia the process shed light on the harm being done by rapid agricultural liberalization and led the government to reintroduce support for some agricultural sectors.[46] But in general the PRSP process, like similar initiatives, has simply not been respected by donors. Conditions continue to appear entirely separately from the PRSP framework. Of the twenty countries with PRSPs completed by March 2003, sixteen had IMF programmes agreed prior to the completion of the PRSP.[47] Even their own independent evaluation bodies found that loans from the international financial institutions (IFIs) informed the PRSP, rather than the other way round.[48] The World Bank actually gives the PRSPs grades. (It has not given a single A grade since 2000, while only five countries have even got Bs.) As one commentator put it, 'Which countries would have signed on to the PRS concept if they knew that rather than the Boards of the IFIs providing broad endorsement of the strategy, they would provide grades?'[49] Another common criticism of PRSPs is that they resemble shopping lists of important policies but lack prioritization to help government decision-making. This suits some donors, who are thus still able to pick and choose which items on the list they will support, while claiming to be supporting government priorities. One donor official accused Cambodia's PRSP of being so broad that only if donors wanted to build 'hotels on the moon' would they fail to find some hook in it that suited their spending priorities.[50]

An indicator of how little progress has been made by the PRSP process is the fact that in 2005, ten years after it was launched, the G8 had to promise once again that 'poor countries must decide and lead their own development strategies and economic policies',[51] implying that this was not presently the case. In fact, promises to reform conditionality are relatively periodic. As far back as 1979 the IMF's *Guidelines on Conditionality* stressed the need to avoid blueprint approaches, pay due regard to the individual political and economic circumstances of particular countries, and keep the number of conditions attached to loans to a minimum.[52] Thirty years later the same promises are still being made. But a quick survey of the world of aid conditionality today shows that, despite the new jargon, little of substance has changed. The following excerpt is taken from the IMF's March 2008 decision to accord Gambia 'Completion Point HIPC' status, allowing it to access much-needed debt relief. It demonstrates how conditionality is enforced:

> Expansionary fiscal and monetary policies and poor governance at the Central Bank of the Gambia (CBG) caused the program supported by the Fund's PRGF [Poverty Reduction and Growth Facility] to go off track. Successful policy adjustments and reform of the CBG led to a new PRGF-supported program in February 2007, and the first review was successfully concluded in August 2007. Earlier attempts to restructure the groundnut sector were unsuccessful. However, in 2007 the government prepared and started implementing a sector reform 'roadmap' to fully liberalize the sector. As part of the roadmap, the government has allowed the free entry of operators at all levels of the value chain and intends to privatize the management of the public groundnut processing plants by 2008.[53]

Under this kind of pressure it is unlikely that Gambia will hold off the liberalization of its groundnut sector for much longer, especially given the country's recent experience of donors cutting off funds when it has followed policies deemed inappropriate.

Some dubbed 2005 the 'Year of Africa'. As campaigners called for more aid, in aid-dependent African countries it was business as usual. In April 2005 Burkina Faso was required to promote private sector participation in the energy sector to secure World Bank money; in August the same year the World Bank and IMF required Mozambique, Ghana and Tanzania to implement a strategy to privatize national banks, while Benin had to show progress in the privatization of its cotton ginneries, telecoms and energy sectors; in October 2005 Rwanda was required to negotiate privatization of its telephone system and tea factories, and to join the East Africa Trade Agreement, to access World Bank finances; and in December 2005 Mali was required to privatize its textile development company and national bank, and

Uganda had to establish a private water supply chain system country-wide.[54] According to Eurodad, a respected network of European NGOs, 71 per cent of World Bank concessional loans and grants remain conditional on sensitive economic reforms, mostly privatization and liberalization, although the World Bank disputes these figures.[55] Some conditions still smack of an absurd desire to micromanage; a condition attached to a loan to Mali insisted that the land management office be moved to the Chief Executive Officer's office.[56]

The number of conditions per World Bank loan rose between 2002 and 2005 from an average of forty-eight to sixty-seven, with privatization conditions rising on average from four to five.[57] The number of IMF conditions per loan remained constant during this period.[58] In 2004–2005, the Ethiopian government needed to complete eighty-five World Bank conditions, while Tanzania had to carry out seventy-eight, not counting all the extra conditions added by bilateral donors.[59] Recent research by the World Bank itself backs up this trend, with an increase in the average amount of benchmarks per loan from thirty to thirty-two between 2005 and 2006. Some assessments have argued that conditions have reduced, but the game being played is a semantic one. While binding conditions have been reduced in some areas, non-binding conditions, or benchmarks, often replace them. While they are supposedly treated differently by donors, recipient governments are sometimes unclear what the difference is and accord them just as much weight. Nor is the number of conditions the only important factor. Ten minor conditions can be less important than one sweeping one. In 2003 one of the conditions on IMF aid to Kenya was the 'implementation of comprehensive trade reforms', which could easily have been ten separate conditions in years past.[60]

The 'good governance' agenda

Today's conditionalities are moving into other areas of political decision-making in part because, after decades of economic liberalization conditions, there is sometimes not much left to liberalize. But the renewed donor focus on how countries are governed has also influenced this new direction. The number of public sector governance conditions as a percentage of overall World Bank lending conditions has increased from 17 per cent in 1995–1999 to 50 per cent in 2007.[61] Even donors that have publicly expressed doubts about economic conditions have backed the move to more governance conditionality. Who could be against good governance? But many fear that while these conditions may appear technical and politically neutral, they are really just more neoliberal conditions through the back door. In some areas, such as competition policy and civil service reform, where blueprints are once again being couriered from Washington, it is not always easy to tell the difference between what is being called 'governance' and what is in fact just more economic policy conditionality.

In most African countries government procurement of services, works and goods makes up a very large part of the budget. It accounts for 70 per cent of Uganda's government expenditure.[62] Worth $2 trillion annually,[63] it is an issue of such political and economic importance to developing countries that they have successfully fought tooth and nail to keep it out of the present round of World Trade Organization (WTO) negotiations, fearing they would be forced to liberalize against their will. But 'good governance' conditions are still pressurizing African countries to reform procurement practices along lines set out by donors. In Sierra Leone a Procurement Act was passed in 2004. The idea for this, according to the World Bank country economist, came from the donors.[64] In 2008 the country faced World Bank pressure to further open up government procurement to competition. Ghana, Rwanda, Tanzania and Uganda, among others, have all introduced new procurement legislation since 2001 in response to World Bank conditions.[65] The new Public Procurement Act in Ghana automatically allows for international competitive bidding for government tenders over a certain size. Originally, the government wanted to restrict smaller projects to local firms, but it capitulated under donor pressure because, according to the

World Bank, limiting participation by nationality 'undermines the principle of transparency and equal opportunity and may be a cause of abuse'.[66]

As with most economic policy decisions, there are pros and cons, winners and losers. Opening up government procurement could reduce corruption and lower costs, and to allow the participation of foreign firms can encourage technology transfer. But governments would also lose a vital tool for intervening in the economy for the benefit of local firms, with consequent impacts on incomes and consumption. In January 2007, a Chinese company won the contract to produce Ghana's fiftieth anniversary cloth. Abraham Koomson, secretary general of the Ghana Federation of Labour, was disappointed: 'If the government had approached local firms just three months earlier, they could have come together to produce all the cloth required.'[67] Jobs for Ghanaians in the textile industry have fallen from 25,000 in 1977 to 7,000 in 1995, to fewer than 3,000 by 2005, as the industry struggles against low-cost imports, smuggling and an influx of second-hand clothes.[68] Like all the issues discussed in this chapter, these are decisions that should rightly be made by sovereign governments, not by donor governments and the international institutions they control, which have clear interests in opening up recipient country markets to foreign competition.

Much of this chapter has criticized the role played by aid donors in setting the policies of sovereign African governments, but it must also be said that donor pressure is sometimes used well. Pressure on countries to reduce human rights violations and to strengthen basic democratic rights exists with or without aid, especially via the UN, but there can be no doubt that threats by donors to withdraw if improvements are not made have been successful in the past. One example is the suspension of aid to Kenya in late 1992 by donors demanding multi-party elections. It worked.[69] Money talks, for both good and bad. Social spending in Benin increased significantly as its donor-approved poverty reduction strategy was implemented after 2000.[70] So while, in my view, donor conditions have harmed Africa overall, there is a debate to be had about where the balance of good and bad lies. What seems fairly certain, though, is that aid conditions, and not the aid money itself, have had the greatest impact on Africa's development in recent decades.

In the balance

In 1995, the World Bank country operations manager for Mozambique told government officials that unless raw cashew exports were allowed, thus ending the protection of national cashew nut processing plants, she would not submit the Country Assistance Strategy to the World Bank Board, which would mean a freezing of aid. Cashews were once Mozambique's largest export, and so the government opposed this policy, aware of the jobs that would be lost. But such threats had been carried out in the past, notably in 1983 and 1986 when food aid had been withheld. The Mozambicans capitulated.[71] By 2001 every large cashew plant had closed, with the loss of 10,000 jobs.[72] 'Ill informed prescriptions by donors often failed because donors did not have a deep understanding of the situation in the recipient country,' was the wry comment of Mozambique's former president, Joaquim Chissano, in an interview in 2007.[73] Did aid work? In the Christmas holidays of 2003 Malawian parliamentarians were called back to approve a bill privatizing the state marketing board and cutting agricultural input subsidies, both preconditions for World Bank lending. According to Collins Magalasi of ActionAid Malawi, 'Because of these conditions thousands of Malawians starved to death.'[74] What were the impacts of aid in Malawi that year? It is a fair question.

What was the impact of aid when user fees were forced on Africa? Can it have been anything but disastrous, despite the fact that some of that aid money was spent on social services as well? What was the impact of aid when the export and financial sectors were liberalized regardless of country context and democratic demands? The British charity Christian Aid estimates that trade liberalization policies as a whole have cost Africa $272 billion since 1985.[75] These are just a few typical examples, and there are many more, of across the board reforms that have utterly changed the African economic landscape. Has it been worth it? Hundreds of billions of dollars in aid at the price of what many consider to be the economic devastation of a continent. A unique initiative involving participants from developing country governments, the World Bank and civil society produced a landmark report which found in 2004 that, 'adjustment policies have contributed to the further impoverishment and marginalisation of local populations, while increasing economic inequality'.[76] Predictably, the World Bank pulled out of the project before these findings were published.

Even if you do not agree, despite the evidence and the growing academic consensus, that these policies have been overwhelmingly harmful, it is clear that they have led to very substantial, long-term, changes across Africa. And this is the point I most want to emphasize. Any assessment of the benefits or otherwise of aid and debt relief must take these complex impacts into account. It is not sensible to focus on aid's direct impacts without also looking at the impacts of the conditions attached. Harmful or helpful, the impacts of aid conditionalities have been far greater than the direct impacts of aid. Many African analysts and civil society leaders have campaigned *against* some aid and debt relief initiatives – not because they are unaware that African governments are in desperate need of cash, but because they are aware of the other side of the coin. Three million people in Mali (whose population is 11 million) depend on a cotton industry that accounts for half of Mali's export earnings. Its privatization is currently a key demand from the World Bank as part of its aid package.[77] Will the possible job losses be worth the cash reward? If privatization is the right thing for the country, shouldn't it be happening anyway? Should Africans continue to agree to this kind of partnership, or is it time to forge a new path?

5 | Institutions, institutions, institutions

In 2003 the Ghanaian parliament approved a new budget which included increases in the import tariffs on rice and poultry. These tariffs were to help local farmers compete with subsidized imports and were fully consistent with (and considerably below) tariff rates allowed by the World Trade Organization's Agreement on Agriculture. However, the government had not negotiated these increases with the IMF prior to finalizing its budget. Following meetings with IMF staff, the government reversed the policy, and stuck with the original, much lower, tariff protection. This was in direct violation of the Ghanaian constitution which stipulates that only the parliament can change a parliament-approved budget. According to Ken Quartey of the Ghana National Association of Poultry Farmers, 'If we become apathetic about voting then it is because only half our leaders are accountable to us. The other half [the IMF, the World Bank and donor governments] are not and if we go down their path and liberalise our economy further, and it doesn't work out, who do we hold to account?'[1]

The previous chapter discussed how aid has affected *what* choices have been made by African countries. But in this chapter I look at the way the donor–recipient relationship affects *how* those choices are made and how recipient countries are run. *What* choice was made in this case? Ghana did not implement the tariffs and the price of chicken has continued to collapse as subsidized European chicken is dumped on Ghana, threatening thousands of livelihoods.[2] Some 97 per cent of poultry is now imported,[3] as is 70 per cent of rice, compared with only 10 per cent twenty years ago.[4] But *how* the choice was made matters just as much. Ghana's developing democracy and public institutions, including its parliament, were undermined because decisions were not taken in the appropriate places, but by donor organizations accountable not to Ghanaians but to the rich countries that finance them. This is a typical example of the sort of donor–recipient relationship that has characterized aid to Africa for many years. And Quartey's reaction is also typical. The aid system, on balance and despite occasionally important interventions in support of democracy, has hindered rather than helped the development of modern political spaces in Africa, and this has meant that citizens find it as hard as ever to claim their political and economic rights. This was not the intention, of course, and at the beginning of the modern era of aid it would have been hard to predict (although some did). But that is how it has turned out.

And it goes even deeper. The sense of powerlessness that has been instilled in governments, the civil service, parliaments and civil society in almost all African countries to varying degrees has led to what might be called the psychological malaise of aid dependence. Aid dependence is not just measurable in terms of aid per GDP. It is apparent in the way governments and other sectors of society go about their business and is characterized by a lack of initiative in developing strategies and policies and, in general, a reactive rather than proactive form of government. Richard Dowden, the director of the Royal African Society, suggests that 'in the long term foreign intervention will undermine Africa's self-respect'.[5]

Accountable and well-run institutions, while never considered *un*important to growth and development, are increasingly considered to be the most important prerequisites for development and poverty reduction in the long term. Although the topic has been discussed for decades, it is sometimes presented today as the latest big idea in development. Everyone is talking about institutions. How do you build them? What kinds are needed? In the 1980s and 1990s, at the height of the neoliberal hegemony, the emphasis was very much on the importance of the private sector and limiting the role played by public institutions and the state in the economy. Now, years of ignoring or attempting to bypass the state have been replaced by efforts to make the state more accountable and more effective. To quote from the Africa Commission, 'Africa's history over the last fifty years has been blighted by two areas of weakness. These have been capacity – the ability to design and deliver policies; and accountability – how well a state answers to its people.'[6] It goes on to call for aid to focus on putting that right. What it does not say is that aid itself has undermined democracy, institutions and the capacity to govern in Africa. This could turn out to be the most serious and long-term impact of aid.

The theory

The failure of the state is often seen as the primary cause of slow development in Africa when compared to other parts of the world such as East Asia, which started from similar levels of poverty in the 1950s and 1960s but has grown impressively since then. Within Africa, the success of Botswana is generally attributed to an unusually well-functioning state bureaucracy and enlightened leadership at the very top. This contrasts with poor and corrupt governance in much of the rest of Africa, sometimes linked to entrenched tribalism. The state has not served the people well and until it is functioning decently, there is little chance of significant improvements in the lives of poor people. The donor community has only recently started making good governance a high priority in its aid giving. As the hubristic neoliberal economic consensus shifts to a slightly more humble approach, the focus on institutions is pervasive. And the thinking is simple: we now admit that we know less than we thought about how development happens, but one thing we do know is that good governance is crucial. The Africa Commission states that, 'Without progress in governance, all other reforms will have limited impact.'[7] This is the modern-day aid consensus. According to the World Bank (in 1994), 'Good governance is epitomized by predictable, open and enlightened policy-making, a bureaucracy imbued with a professional ethos acting in furtherance of the public good, the rule of law, transparent processes, and a strong civil society participating in public affairs. Poor governance (on the other hand) is characterized by arbitrary policy making, unaccountable bureaucracies, unenforced or unjust legal systems, the abuse of executive power, a civil society unengaged in public life, and widespread corruption.'[8] The overwhelming burden to improve governance is on African governments and people themselves. Sustained change can only come from within. But donors want to help too.

Overall, the focus on institutions is a positive development, despite the reservations about the 'good governance' agenda explained in the last chapter. Institutions do need to be well resourced in order to work effectively. Just as it is hard to see how an education system could develop successfully without investment, it is hard to imagine a good system of governance developing in a context of chronic lack of funds. The contribution of foreign aid to simply maintaining a functioning and paid civil service in many African countries has clearly been significant. In many countries employees in civil institutions, such as judges and other members of the legal machinery, are trained and remunerated with foreign aid. The World Bank alone furnished Africa with seventy civil service reform projects between 1987 and 1997, while about a quarter of the bank's credits to Africa are for capacity building.[9] There appears to be some consensus regarding the improved management of central banks in Africa, partly a result of foreign pressure and advice. It is also possible that if public sector wages increase as a consequence of aid, more competent people are attracted to the civil service, and incentives for bribe-taking are reduced, further complementing improved governance (although IMF aid conditions have played a role in keeping down public sector wages in Africa). A report on technical assistance by the European Court of Auditors found that only 'one-third of [European Commission] projects have been, or are likely to be, successful in reaching their objectives', but it is also likely that some of the many efforts at 'capacity building' over the years have paid off.[10]

Donors are using traditional methods in their push to improve governance in Africa, drastically increasing the governance content of the conditions attached to aid. About 50 per cent of World Bank aid conditions now relate to public sector governance, compared with 17 per cent at the end of the 1990s, and this ratio is particularly high in Africa compared with other regions.[11] Most of the conditions relate to public financial management, civil service reform, tax issues, accountability, anti-corruption and legal reform. There is less focus on transparency in government decision-making, public access to documents and support for free and independent media.[12] Those seeking to distance themselves from conventional conditions include governance criteria in their selectivity analyses. The World Bank allocates aid according to how well countries perform on its Country Policy and Institutional Assessment (CPIA). The CPIA includes five criteria relating to how public institutions operate, looking at accountability, corruption, property rights, efficiency and financial management, among other things. If a country scores well on these it is likely to see aid increases; if it scores badly it will find it harder to access funds from the World Bank and those donors (the majority) that rely on the bank's analysis to make their own decisions about where to target aid. More than $4 billion of aid was spent on 'improving government administration' in 2005.[13]

It is possible that some of these governance conditionalities will have positive results in the short term and lend weight to the progressive sectors of government and civil society who want to see more accountability. Donor pressure to involve civil society more in decision-making has had important results in some countries, where civil society has grown stronger, although in others, such as Kenya, civil society remains unengaged in these processes.[14] In some cases the overriding of state institutions by outside actors may be the right thing to do. In 2000 the IMF withheld an aid credit from Kenya after the country's High Court ruled the important Anti-Corruption Authority (created three years earlier) unconstitutional.[15] It is clear why a donor would feel the need to halt aid in this way. So those that point to the important contribution of aid to African institutions are not entirely misguided. But governance conditions and the presence of large amounts of aid money can have negative impacts, too. In the case of the Kenyan High Court, the trade-off for donors stepping in was the undermining of a key pillar of Kenya's struggling democracy. Following this episode Kenya's Attorney General drafted a bill which he showed the IMF for approval before it was tabled in parliament. The fundamental contradiction that few donors appear prepared squarely to face is that the more they involve themselves in governance issues in Africa, however well intentioned, the more harm they may be doing to the strengthening of institutions. Rwanda's administrative capacity has significantly increased since the genocide in 1994, thanks in part to donor collaboration. But this has led to more, not less, donor involvement in policymaking and budgeting, which is itself a problem. A report looking at donor–government relations in Rwanda talks of the 'perverse outcomes of an aid system which aims at increasing local ownership but which leads to heightened external entanglement in internal policy processes', noting that the 'ensuing encroachment upon national sovereignty, power and control has raised concern in Rwanda'.[16]

Policymaking capacity

Let us take the case of Zambia.[17] Since the World Bank first became heavily involved in setting Zambian economic policy in 1983, the country has been the recipient of the usual recipe of reform being implemented across Africa. The ruling party in the 1980s was not totally against the kind of economic reforms being insisted on by the World Bank, but Zambian leaders were concerned that they should be allowed to modify the package to suit the political climate. Opposition parties and trade unions were rising up against very unpopular measures that would mean short-term pain for a hoped-for long-term gain. But when in 1987 the government sought to make some changes in the Structural Adjustment Programme signed with the World Bank, including a reintroduction of some import controls and a limitation of debt-service to 10 per cent of export earnings (this was before donors finally accepted that debt needed to be cancelled), the bank simply refused. The IFIs cut off all funding to Zambia and ensured that other donors did the same until eighteen months later the government was so short of money it had to re-engage with donors, which meant reversing its previous decisions and, among other things, freeing up food prices and removing food subsidies. The government had tried to function as it should, as most democratic governments do, but it was not allowed to.

The pattern was repeated fifteen years later with a new government, more donor rhetoric about ownership, but similar consequences. Following large-scale protests against the proposed privatizations of the state-owned commercial bank and electricity provider, required by donors as part of a debt relief package, a parliamentary motion in December 2002 demanded a rethink. President Mwanawasa responded by promising a renegotiation with the IFIs to keep the enterprises in state hands. The IMF responded by announcing that Zambia would forfeit $1 billion in debt relief if the privatization of the bank didn't go ahead. The IMF resident representative had a simple message: 'If they don't sell, they will not get the money.'[18] In February 2003 Mwanawasa said that the IMF privatization programme in Zambia 'has been of no significant benefit to the country ... privatization of crucial state enterprises has led to poverty, asset stripping and job losses'.[19] What have such experiences contributed over the past thirty years to the capacity of African governments to govern well?

In 1995 a report commissioned by the Tanzanian government into its relations with donors judged the relationship to be dominated by 'intrusive donor conditionality' and called for major shifts to allow Tanzania to take a lead in policymaking. It noted the 'relative passivity of the government in the face of multiple donors', although it suggested that the government could be more proactive in seeking to set the agenda.[20] Twelve years later, after a decade during which Tanzania has often been held up as an example of how donors and recipients can work well together, a recent study argues that 'it is hard to discern a contemporary

CCM [Chama Cha Mapinduzi, the revolutionary party, in power in various guises since independence] political project which is distinct from the consensus view of development policy held by the majority of donors'.[21] Some might argue that Tanzania has been increasingly successful at bringing donors on board with its views and strategies, and there is certainly evidence that on some issues Tanzania has been able to oppose donors and win (for instance when it reversed the decision to privatize water supply in Dar es Salaam).[22] Unfortunately, the opposite view is more likely: the Tanzanian government is not leading but following and is developing policies which respond to what it knows to be donor preferences. The same study found some insiders who thought Tanzania was standing up to donors, but others identified a 'policy vacuum' at the heart of government.[23]

Studies in other countries have drawn similar conclusions. Ghana's budget has been described as a 'façade' and a 'deceptive mirage' directed towards satisfying donors rather than being a genuine and thought-through spending plan.[24] A 2007 analysis of aid's impacts in Mali talks of 'a mentality of aid dependency' in the country, restricting the 'world of the possible' and leading to the loss of the 'habit, capacity, and incentives to set up and implement their own policies'. It describes the Malian government as having 'adopted a strategy of compliance aimed at maximizing aid flows coming into the country', and argues that 'aid is not a mere financial and technical tool to support national initiatives: it has replaced any national political reflection on development in the country'.[25] In Mozambique the first Action Plan to Reduce Absolute Poverty (PARPA 2001–2005), which is the country's key policy document, was unashamedly guided by donor strategies. The second PARPA (2006–2010) was heavily influenced by foreign consultants and was not even shown to the parliament, although donors, of course, were invited to comment.[26] In an analysis of aid to Sierra Leone, not one expert interviewed could think of an example of the government refusing aid because it was opposed to the terms on offer.[27]

All of which is disappointing, but hardly surprising. We have seen how often policies developed nationally have simply been rejected by donors. While on the one hand donors emphasize the need to listen to country governments and civil society, which is acknowledged as vital for policies to work, on the other they make clear that certain policy options are out of bounds. Over time recipient governments have learnt to play the role cut out for them. The problem of self-censorship now pervades African government policymaking. When countries know they will not have a chance of passing a particular law, or will have to spend immense political capital trying to get it past donors, they may not bother to think about it, let alone suggest it. In Mozambique an attempt by the government to take the policy initiative with the launch of a development bank met flat rejection from donors (despite the usual rhetoric encouraging policy autonomy and ownership).[28] When even flagship government projects like this are blocked by donors, how many projects do countries simply not bother to develop into proposals? In a context of donor pressure to liberalize and privatize, what recipient country would put forward a plan for increased subsidies and nationalization, even if it considered such measures to be in the best interests of the country? A study of twenty-three Poverty Reduction Strategy Papers in 2001 concluded that they clearly reflected policies endorsed strongly by the World Bank and IMF.[29] According to the study of aid to Mali, 'As aid-donors' influence over policy has increased, [Mali's] capacity and will to take the lead in managing aid and the aid relationship have decreased. Indeed, if the current political situation seems characterized by a certain degree of inertia, a lack of development strategy, weak capacities and compliance with donors, it can only be understood as the result of the weakening of the state and donor entanglement in national institutions and politics, and several decades of aid dependence.'[30] In the words of one civil society leader from Niger, 'We have become aid economies; we no longer know how to reflect on the solutions we need to put in place in our countries.'[31]

The will of the people?

Government capacity, its ability to plan and develop coherent policies, is undermined by dependence on aid. But what is the role of ordinary people in all this? If constantly responding to donor pressure has made African governments less effective, what has it meant for democracy and the accountability of the state to its citizens? The need for effective states is obvious. The state carries out functions vital to growth and development, so underperforming officials in ineffective bureaucracies will clearly harm the chances of progress. But the need for accountability is less clear. Many countries developed their economies successfully under authoritarian regimes (Singapore and Korea being the best examples), while today's China, whose economy is growing very rapidly, remains a highly authoritarian one-party state. As Matthew Lockwood remarks in his important book *The State They're In*, 'Authoritarian rule seems to produce developmental outcomes that are either very good or very bad; democratic rule tends to languish in the middle.'[32] In Africa it is hard to find an example of authoritarian rule that has achieved 'very good' outcomes, though there are quite a few examples of the opposite. The development of representative government in most countries in the world has been the most important means of allowing poor people more power over decisions that affect them – the power to vote for someone else or the opportunity to meet and influence their representatives. This is surely one of the most vital dynamics that Africans must foster if they are to cut poverty in the short and, more realistically, long term. Accountability is not only important for governments but also for basic service providers. The World Bank's 2004 World Development Report on basic services developed a helpful framework that emphasized the importance of accountability of service providers, be they public or private, to the user. The longer the chain of accountability, the report argued, the less chance the consumer has of a good service.[33] Poor people have always found it harder than rich people to have their voices heard, and that is unlikely to change. But when effective accountability mechanisms are in place, the poor have more chance of having their concerns listened to and addressed. Unfortunately, aid has, on balance, played a hindering role in the development of participation and accountability in Africa, and continues to do so.

Parliaments are never perfect. It takes years of trial and error for them to function well, and even then there are always problems. The presence of corruption in the US Congress is well known and appears endemic. So are similar concerns throughout the developed parliamentary democracies of western Europe, with Jacques Chirac of France and Silvio Berlusconi of Italy the most recent presidents to be embroiled in corruption charges. Yet such problems should not obscure the basic importance of elected representation. Almost everyone would agree that a functioning parliament is vital for a modern state with aspirations to growth, equity and development. Although substantial quantities of aid are spent supporting parliaments, experience shows that their worth has been repeatedly undermined by the government–donor nexus. Donors have frequently shown themselves to be more interested in what they consider to be the right policies than allowing parliaments the space they need to develop as decision-making bodies. The reordering of government away from the people and towards donors has grave implications for the development of an accountable state. While aid cannot be entirely to blame it has exacerbated a situation in which politicians and bureaucrats do not concern themselves with developing state–citizen accountability.

The fact that governments feel more accountable to donors than to their own parliaments and people dominates attempts by civil society to stand up for its interests. African civil society has responded in many instances by linking up with international NGOs to try to get a foot in the door at donor capitals like Washington, Geneva and London, not without success, especially on single issues like HIV/AIDS. But this does little to support the development of national-level decision-making processes. Moreover, there are fewer and fewer political options available to the citizenry – all parties have to adhere to donor thinking to obtain funding. So where is the choice at the ballot box? Opposition to the Zambian government's neoliberal policies in the second half of the 1980s was led by the trade union leader Frederick Chiluba. However, when Chiluba was elected president in 1991, rather than change the course of economic policy in the country, he took liberalization to an even more radical phase. According to one substantial analysis of this period, 'the MMD's (Movement for Multi-party Democracy) "strategy" was essentially to place economic decision-making in the hands of IFI staff, believing that they had access to expertise that Zambia did not ...'[34] Between 1991 and 1996 the World Bank and IMF gave eight loan packages between them and attached the usual conditions, including liberalizing agricultural markets and labour laws, cutting the civil service, increasing social spending and formulating policies on privatization.[35] In this context, is democracy functioning in any real sense?

Donor attempts to involve civil society more and support national ownership of policymaking have often been perfectly genuine. Some see this as a way of making concrete changes in the direction of policy; for others it is just a way to get more support for the same policies. The PRSP process became the name of the game in many African countries in the late 1990s, and it remains the dominant methodology behind these efforts. It is meant to enhance government and citizen ownership of policies by sitting them both down with donors to work on joint proposals. On the whole it hasn't worked. In fact, in some countries it has signified another step away from real democracy: whoever you vote for, you get the same thing. A civil society that is not necessarily representative is standing in for formal political processes. This is not an accident; it is a central part of the PRSP methodology. As the Zambian PRSP was being put together in 2000 all sectors of society were invited to help influence it except political parties and, again, parliament, which was not shown the document either for discussion or approval. Parliamentarians were invited to two informal workshops along with representatives of civil society, although few attended – many had not even heard of the process.

With an election looming in 2001, donors were keen that the document should not be associated with the current government – otherwise it would have to be redrafted in the event of a different government getting elected. In 2004 the Minister of Finance said, 'We are running the country but the budget is controlled by donors.'[36] Rather than strengthening democracy, the PRSP process organized by aid donors delegitimized the democratic process, relegating elected representatives to observers. This type of consensus-based policymaking takes the politics out of democracy. Removing ideological and policy differences does nothing to reduce, and could even promote, the tribal and ethnic divisions which continue to play a deep role in African political allegiances, as the turmoil in Kenya in early 2008 once again demonstrated. And not only do citizens lose what trust they might have had in their ability to influence their governments, as Ken Quartey suggested at the beginning of this chapter, but the nature of people entering politics may even change, with people motivated by a desire to change things (why bother?) being replaced by people seeking a slice of the government cake.

The processes of state consolidation hoped for and to a certain extent achieved in Africa after independence have suffered setbacks since the 1980s. There is an anecdote about how one African head of state was so annoyed with donor complaints about civil rights in his country that he threatened to reverse recent reforms.[37] This sort of threat only makes sense if reforms are 'owned' by donors rather than national governments. Political negotiations of this kind between donors and recipients do not bolster the accountability and credibility of the state. By comparison, when governments negotiate seriously with domestic constituents, progress is made. When successive governments of Mauritius have found themselves involved in difficult bargaining with sugar producers, the process has probably been tiring and testing. But it contributed to the building of what is an increasingly effective and accountable state. Learning by doing, even if you get it wrong, is a vital and overlooked part of state-building.[38]

Parallel development

A large amount of aid is spent outside recipient governments' budgets. Donors set up parallel structures to spend the money, employing their own staff, writing their own rules, developing their own set of contacts and contracts. Less than 40 per cent of aid to governments uses recipient country public financial management and procurement systems, and less than 60 per cent of aid from the African Development Bank was even recorded in recipient government budgets.[39] The benefits of setting up parallel systems are clear – fast results managed by donors who want to see fast results. But there are downsides. Multiple channels make it harder for governments to achieve anything resembling policy coherence and make basic accounting much harder, if not impossible. In Malawi donors have established sixty-nine 'project units', almost half of which are run by the United States Agency for International Development (USAID).[40] Because Sierra Leone's Decentralization Secretariat is primarily funded by the World Bank it is very well resourced, but this also means that it is more accountable to the World Bank than to its host, the poorly resourced Ministry of Local Governance. According to some critics, it has failed to take into consideration existing local political structures as it pushes decentralization. Donors in Sierra Leone have been accused of setting up local units to interact with local communities 'in utter negligence of the actual power structures on the ground', and of imagining the communities as 'a power-free, harmonious universe'.[41]

The direct benefits of aid-supported health programmes are partly offset by more negative effects on health systems as a whole. A particular problem is that of vertical disease-specific programmes supported by donors, which tend to fragment health systems, emphasize donor not country priorities, and attract already scarce health professionals away from the national health system. This appears to be a particular problem in HIV programmes, a donor priority. Rwanda only has a 3 per cent HIV/AIDS prevalence rate – low for Africa. The Rwandan health strategy emphasizes the need to improve health systems and essential services for a country where infant mortality is still 118 per 1,000 and maternal mortality 1,400 per 100,000. Nevertheless, the country receives $46 million to fight HIV/AIDS and only $1 million for the integrated management of childhood illnesses (IMCI). Only 14 per cent of total donor support for health is spent through the Rwandan Ministry of Health, with a further 12 per cent going to local governments. The rest is directly managed by the donors or goes to the NGOs they work with.[42] The budget for the US's flagship vertical fund, the PEPFAR HIV/AIDS programme, was 125 per cent of the Mozambican government's total health budget in 2006, and none of it was spent using national systems.[43] The World Bank does little better; only a quarter of its aid to Mozambique uses government systems.[44]

The anti-state ideology of the 1980s and 1990s hindered the development of strong systems. Although today the battle regarding the importance of the state appears to have been won, it is not easy to repair two decades of undermining of ministries and civil servants. Planning and budgeting functions, in particular, have been impaired, in part because of the donor drive to slim down African civil services. According to a former director at Mali's Ministry of Planning, 'Instead of being extended to all ministries, the planning units that used to exist and were very efficient in key ministries (agriculture, health, education), were completely dismantled in 1989.'[45] Between 1987 and 1989 one in five of Malian civil servants (about 10,000 people) were made redundant.[46] It takes time to rebuild capacity after such drastic reductions, and the social costs can also be high. In Togo in 1996, half the households of retrenched civil servants withdrew one or more child from school.[47]

Capacity development has also been undermined, ironically, by technical assistance intended to develop capacity. Most African civil servants have stories about the 'experts' sent by donors to 'assist' with policymaking, money spending and other government processes. The OECD estimates that spending on technical assistance, mostly foreign advisers shipped in from the donor country, accounts for half of all aid, and in Zambia more money is received in the form of technical assistance than is spent by the government each year on education.[48] Donor experts often follow donor priorities more than those of the host government. The advice given by donor-paid experts has been so integral to changing policies in recipient countries that one of the main strategies being adopted by the Zambian government in its attempt to regain control of policymaking after years of an effective abdication of planning is to limit discussions with donors and donor-financed technical advisers.[49] While the presence of foreigners can be useful at times, it has long since become a business in its own right. According to a civil society representative in Niger, 'after more than 40 years, technical assistance is more part of the problem than the solution'.[50] Rather than building capacity it more often than not compensates for the lack of it. Jobs that donors want to prioritize are done in the short term, but development of long-term capacity is further undermined. Ethiopia has long annoyed donors by refusing many offers of technical assistance for precisely this reason.[51]

In many cases experienced civil servants are tempted away from serving the state to work for donors at much higher salaries, debilitating state bureaucracies in the short and long term.[52] The erosion of public finances, fiscal constraints and public sector wage caps – direct results of donor conditions – have made it even harder for governments to keep hold of the best and brightest. In Mozambique the World Bank paid for the most promising civil service economists to do Masters courses overseas, then gave the best ones jobs in the local World Bank office.[53] Like so many of aid's problems, no one planned it that way, but this is how it has turned out.

When you devise a strategy you need to know how much money you have got to spend. If you don't, or if the number keeps changing, it makes planning ahead very difficult. Lack of certainty at government level filters down to where it really matters, with schools and hospitals unable to plan the year ahead because they don't know what money they will have. Volatility and unpredictability is one of aid's defining characteristics and is the result of conditionality and bureaucracy. When countries fail to complete targets and benchmarks, aid can be cut off. In 2007, when the IMF announced that fiscal targets in Sierra Leone had not been met, the European Commission, World Bank and the Department for International Development (DFID) halted their budget support payments.[54] In 2006 donor bureaucracy meant that less than 50 per cent of committed aid was disbursed in Sierra Leone.[55] Other countries fared a lot better, with Ghana's aid receipts varying only by about 5 per cent from what has been agreed.[56]

Other foreign flows are unpredictable as well: foreign investment depends as much on external factors beyond a government's control as they do on government policy. Domestic revenue, too, can vary. But ODA to Africa is four times more volatile than government revenue.[57] Donors' promises are simply unreliable. Despite having pledged to double aid by 2010 Italy's aid fell by 30 per cent in 2006, while Japan is also breaking its promise to raise aid. According to UNCTAD, 'increases in aid to specific countries have not usually been sustained for more than a few years'.[58] That aid flows are unstable is not a good reason to decrease them, but it implies that African governments should not rely on them too much, particularly for vital or core expenses. A World Bank assessment of aid effectiveness found that most donors give aid to Rwanda, for instance, on an annual or biannual basis and that this leads to 'substantial variations in the level of funding from year to year', inhibiting long-term planning.[59] High turnover of donor staff is another problem. According to one Ethiopian government official, 'We feel we've agreed policies, and then someone comes three weeks later and says it's awful.'[60]

Aid and corruption

The relationship between aid and corruption has been the subject of hot debate, with donors highlighting the fight against corruption as a focus for their efforts. That corruption is a chronic problem in most African countries is well known; in some countries it is perhaps the major political issue. It is to be expected that some aid funds, just like other funds, are lost to corruption. But this is not a reason to give less aid – it might even be a good reason to give more aid. If a percentage of money is diverted away by corruption then increasing aid, while increasing the amount of money lost, will probably also increase the part that is spent well. But our question is different, not whether aid goes missing (it does) but whether aid tends to reduce or increase corruption in Africa, and whether increased aid might have positive or negative consequences.

There are clear examples of aid donors playing an important role in fighting corruption. The World Bank and other donors have encouraged the refusal of public contracts to companies which have bribed government officials.[61] Gordon Brown may have been exaggerating when he went so far as to call for 'corruption-free regimes',[62] but donors are certainly spending time and money supporting the development of better public finance management systems. Some of their efforts have paid off.

Unfortunately, plenty of examples also exist of aid fuelling corruption, with Mobutu's Zaire being only the most extreme and infamous example. The simple availability of large amounts of aid not only fed corruption but created it, just as large amounts of oil or other natural resource profits often have done. Aid can lead to corruption when there is urgent pressure to disburse large amounts of money without proper oversight mechanisms being in place, or when reforms such as downsizing the public sector or privatizing national companies are pushed through too fast. There is strong evidence that donor obsession with quick privatizations in Mozambique, for instance, especially of the banking sector, caused the corrupting of a previously relatively healthy civil service and private sector, the pickings being so great and the oversight so theoretical. The World Bank, it is claimed, preferred to turn a blind eye to corruption as long as privatizations were pushed through.[63] That aid conditionality is responsible for the corrupting of a political generation is a very grave charge, though it appears to be quite plausible. The consequences of such a worsening in the governance situation of a country are likely to be long term and hard to reverse, and they need to be taken very seriously when we are analysing the overall impact of aid. Research carried out in 2007 suggested that up to 50 per cent of aid to post-conflict countries is lost to corruption, fuelling dangerous public resentment, while donor-established parallel operating units tolerate patronage and undermine the emergence of accountable institutions.[64] But overall there does not appear to be a significant generalized relationship between aid and increasing corruption – the evidence is mixed. In another of these endless and probably dubious regressions foisted on the world by economists, Alberto Alesina and Beatrice Weder find that high levels of corruption within recipient countries were positively correlated with aid flows throughout the 1990s.[65] But, as usual, others have claimed to show the opposite.[66]

Keeping people in power

The most extreme way that aid can undermine accountability is when it actually succeeds in keeping a particular person or party in power or, conversely, plays a role in getting rid of them. A basic measure of accountability is that when a regime fails it falls. Given the deep economic decline Africa has experienced since the early 1980s, one might expect a reasonably fast turnover of leaders. But when it comes to staying-power, African leaders lead the world. Since 1980, African leaders have stayed in power an average of twelve years, three times longer than the Western average. According to one analysis, 'The absence of accountability is then not a manner of speech, but a practical reality: it is literally true that African governments avoid accountability for their performance.'[67] How? Because when economic policies fail, aid steps in to soften the blow. The most recent example of this is Zimbabwe, where aid has helped Robert Mugabe keep his grip on power. In 2001, as hunger spread and the country geared up for elections, the UN's World Food Programme and other agencies stepped in to help feed millions of Zimbabweans. Robert Mugabe won the election and continued his failed policies. Did food aid play a part in keeping Mugabe in power for another seven years?

Quite possibly. Should donors intervene in emergencies to help people who are facing terrible hardship? In general, yes. It is hard to know the right thing to do. But what is clear is that if we are trying to evaluate the impact of aid to Zimbabwe we need to look at its indirect as well as its direct impacts.[68]

Humanitarian concerns are not always top of the list for donors. Foreign powers have often played an insidious role in African democracy, using aid to get their favoured leaders into government and keep them in power, regardless of whether they are benefiting the country and impervious to the wishes of the people. The lengthy career of Zaire's dictator, Mobutu Sese Seko, was possible only because of constant support from the West as part of the Cold War. But it is not just the villains who have been helped to stay in power by aid. When an African economy suffers a downturn, or decisions are made to strengthen the army rather than basic services, for example, the consequences a normal government might experience are dampened because aid steps in. This is one of the reasons why favoured African leaders, such as Yoweri Museveni of Uganda, Meles Zenawi of Ethiopia and Benjamin Mkapa of Tanzania, have done so well, to name just three. On the positive side of the scales, the power of aid can also play a part in boosting democracy. According to some analyses, Mali's structural adjustment programmes (for all the harm they may have done) may have been decisive in the fall of the military regime in the early 1990s as they forced the break-up of the clientelist system and fomented calls for democratization.[69] The nature of a government, particularly the president or prime minister, is far more important than the usual impacts of aid for a country's overall development prospects. If the provision of aid succeeds in keeping a leader or government in power or if its cutting off leads a government to collapse, the impact of that aid on the citizens of that country is unquantifiably big.

No representation without taxation

This chapter has outlined a number of ways in which aid has undermined the development of accountable and effective state institutions in Africa. The basic problem is intrinsic. Governments and decision-makers, like the rest of us, pay most heed to the people with the money. The problem is similar in countries that rely heavily on oil or natural resource revenues for their income, such as Nigeria and Angola, which receive very little aid and where there has long been criticism that oil companies are listened to before the concerns of citizens. In the Middle East oil-dependent states have resisted pressures to democratize, helped by the fact they have no need to tax anyone. Some historians attribute the slower development of the Spanish Cortes in relation to the English parliament in the sixteenth and seventeenth centuries to the huge windfall revenues accruing to monarchs from gold and silver from the Americas.[70] Like any windfall to governments, foreign aid reduces the importance of domestic revenue and therefore the vital 'social contract' of accountability between government and people. Governments that receive large amounts of external financing will worry less about support at home and have less need to defend their decisions and promote popular participation in the workings of government. Meanwhile, citizens who know that policy is made to please donors and not them are likely to spend less time trying to pressure their governments to change – what's the point? A famous saying from the American Revolution is 'No taxation without representation', but the converse is also true. Without taxation, or when taxes paid by citizens are relatively less important, effective representation can remain far off.

The obvious way to improve state accountability is to increase tax revenue in relation to aid. The role played by taxes in the relationship between state and citizen has been fundamental throughout history according to those who study the development of the modern state: 'The evolution of democracy and the rule of law in the West was critically related to monarchs' needs for tax revenues, particularly for fighting wars. Elites who provided monarchs with most of their tax revenues in turn demanded accountability from government. Accountability was gradually extended from the elite to the people at large. England is the prototypical example, with the Magna Carta and the Glorious Revolution being two of the most prominent events in the process of increasing accountability of monarchs to elites, followed eventually by gradual extension of the suffrage.'[71]

From a historical perspective, state accountability has grown side by side with taxation. Conversely, when a large proportion of the money needed by the state is available from a source other than its citizens, the development of state accountability is retarded. Overall, African countries continue to take far less in tax revenue than developed countries, with a tax to GDP ratio of only 16 per cent in 2005 (discounting South Africa).[72] This is partly explained by high levels of poverty and subsistence and large agricultural and informal sectors. Nevertheless, it is hard to find anyone who disagrees that they should be seeking to increase tax revenue as a share of government revenue, not only to improve the accountability of state institutions, but also for reasons of basic fiscal sustainability – aid will not last for ever (or so it is assumed) and one day taxes will have to take over. The question is, do high aid receipts make it less likely that governments will raise taxes?

Intuitively, one would assume that receiving high levels of aid is a disincentive to seeking to increase domestic revenue. As any politician knows, raising taxes is not an easy thing to do, and the availability of aid militates against these politically difficult decisions being taken. There is considerable evidence to back up this view. Very few countries in the world have both high levels of aid receipts and high levels of tax collection. According to a recent survey of the evidence, most studies find that the impact of aid on fiscal revenues is either negative or insignificant.[73] Aid conditionalities in this area, as in others, may have worsened the situation. Adjustment policies have frequently been responsible for reductions in formal sector unemployment and therefore the erosion of the income tax revenue base. Employment in the Kenyan public sector (taxable) declined from 30 per cent of total employment in 1990 to 11 per cent in 2000, while formal private sector jobs (taxable) also halved from 36.5 per cent of total employment to 17 per cent over the same period. Meanwhile, employment in the non-agricultural informal sector (hard to tax) tripled in Kenya between 1990 and 2000, from about 23 per cent of total employment to 70 per cent.[74]

However, the evidence is mixed. Case studies of Ghana and Malawi actually show aid having a positive impact on revenue collection, while in Zambia the impact appears to have been negative.[75] Two multi-country studies from the IMF starkly contradict each other. In one analysis of the impact of foreign aid in 107 countries between 1970 and 2000, grant aid was found to dampen revenue collection efforts, especially in very corrupt countries where 'the decline in revenues completely offsets the increase in grants'. The impact of concessional loans, however, was positive on revenue mobilization, which the authors put down to governments concentrating on mobilizing higher revenues in preparation for future debt repayments.[76] However, a more recent study found precisely the opposite: foreign aid improves revenue performance in low-income countries, while debt financing leads to a decline in revenues, though not a very significant one.[77]

There have been some encouraging signs in Africa since 2002, with domestic revenue climbing as a percentage of GDP for the first time in a long while, especially for those countries that are predominantly oil exporters, but also for oil importers.[78] If other revenues increase faster than aid, dependency on aid will decrease, taking African governments one step closer to resolving some of the problems of capacity and accountability outlined in this chapter. So these gains are important. But, unfortunately, they are fragile. Today's higher tax revenues are largely a result of sharp increases in commodity prices, especially oil and minerals. With the prospect of a global slowdown, it is far from assured that high prices will last, and revenue gains in many countries could be reversed. If aid rises at the rate campaigners are demanding and governments are promising it will almost certainly outpace revenue collection efforts in most African countries. Based on the evidence it is hard to generalize about whether aid helps or hinders tax collection efforts, or whether grants help and loans do not, or vice versa. It probably depends, like most things, on the government concerned. Some countries may be able to sustain revenue growth and therefore hold off the negative impacts of aid on state capacity and accountability. Grant aid may be useful in some countries when it reduces the need for borrowing, for example. But for others, which may have had the opportunity to pull themselves out of aid dependency, the danger is of a reversal. For some African countries, like Ethiopia, that have managed to retain strong institutional capacity as well as decision-making responsibility, increased aid may threaten this sovereignty. What we need is a differentiated approach, taking into account the complexities of aid giving and the risks to development that might occur if ratios of aid to government revenue deteriorate further in Africa. But what we have are generalized calls for aid increases across the board which do not take these concerns seriously.

Like the policy impacts of aid conditionality, the impacts of aid on state institutions and accountable governance have been severe and long term. They are certainly among the most important impacts that aid giving has had in Africa. Some analysts have even linked aid conditionality and structural adjustment policies to the promotion of conflict on the continent.[79] What is clear is that aid dependency has become a serious problem for most African countries. The fundamental problems associated with aid and accountability are unlikely to be resolved in the new era of aid, and may worsen, despite efforts by donors to press for more accountable governance. Is giving more aid the answer, or is it time to start the process of reducing aid in some circumstances? Ravi Kanbur, a former chief economist for Africa at the World Bank, is one respected analyst who argues that 'a reduced volume of conventional development aid to Africa [is] a price worth paying for reduced aid dependence'.[80]

6 | Aid, growth and confused academics

We have looked at three major categories of impact: direct, policy and institutional. While the direct impacts of aid are mixed, with some positive and some negative, the impacts on policies and institutions have been mostly negative and will probably worsen as aid continues to rise. There is one area we have not yet looked at which may explain why, in the face of this evidence, aid's proponents remain so optimistic. Economic growth is considered by most people to be a prerequisite for poverty reduction, and the relationship between aid and growth is one of the most researched topics in development. Aid's proponents argue that it will lead to growth. The thinking behind the new era of aid is well summed up by Britain's Prime Minister, Gordon Brown: 'The success of aid will be measured not in pounds spent by donors, but in the rates of growth and poverty reduction achieved by recipients.'[1] But there are problems. First, the links between the two objectives are complex: growth does not necessarily lead to poverty reduction, and we should be much more interested in the welfare and rights of poor people than the overall financial status of a country. Second, the evidence suggesting that aid foments growth is riddled with methodological problems and is balanced by similar amounts of contradictory evidence.

Growth does not equal poverty reduction

While almost all economists believe that economic growth is an important ingredient in poverty reduction, it is by no means all that is required. It is perfectly possible for a country's economy to grow year on year over a long period with minimal changes in the poverty rate – this happens quite regularly. In Tanzania, for example, GDP grew by an average of about 4 per cent a year between 1990 and 2000, but the proportion of people living below the national poverty line fell only slightly. With a population growth rate of about 3 per cent a year that meant that there were more poor people in Tanzania by the end of the decade, despite economic growth.[2] Africa is the only region in the world where the absolute number of people below the $1-a-day poverty line has been steadily rising in recent years.[3] More children were in school in Tanzania by the end of the 1990s, and more people had clean water, but the number of children dying before the age of five had gone up and the proportion of the population with HIV or AIDS had doubled to over 12 per cent.[4]

It is possible that, over time, growth will lead to poverty reduction, but it matters how and where that growth is taking place. Mozambique is growing fast, yet many Mozambicans will tell you they are getting poorer – the huge Mozal aluminium smelter contributes to economic growth statistics but not very much to the lives of ordinary people. Angola is another good example. Like Mozambique, it grew at a rate of 7–8 per cent per year between 1998 and 2006, faster than the regional average. But the dominance of the offshore oil sector, and its complete separation from the rest of the economy, means that growth in its GDP bears little or no relation to the living conditions of its population. According to UNCTAD, 'Recent economic growth [in Africa] has not translated into corresponding increases in employment, and the limited job creation that has taken place has mainly been in the informal sector, due to the capital-intensive and enclave nature of the extractive sectors that have been driving this growth.'[5] It goes on to say that the problem of 'jobless growth' is a serious concern for African governments.[6] Growth in the agricultural sector, on which most poor people in Africa depend, would lead to far more poverty reduction for many more people.

It is often said that without growth it is hard to see how space can be created for poverty reduction. This is probably true. If poverty is not reducing in conditions of economic growth it is difficult to envisage how it will reduce in a recession. Richer people have ways to stave off financial ruin that poor people do not. But poverty reduction dependent on the trickle-down of wealth in a growing economy is very fragile – it does little to change the structural reasons why people are poor and will not survive an economic downturn. Equality matters too. In countries with more social inequality it is more likely that growth will benefit the few and not the majority. In Namibia, a country with very high levels of inequality, the financial sector does not cater to the needs of the urban poor and rural populations, who therefore find it harder to save for the future. Moreover, as their savings are not being productively invested, the economy as a whole loses out.[7] Certain types of growth common under the neoliberal model exacerbate inequality even further, with the rich people's incomes growing at a much faster rate than those of the poor. Apart from being unfair, this can make life worse for poor people when it leads to inflation in the prices of goods and services that were previously affordable. Inequality is a key source of tension and social conflict in a society, often linked with higher crime rates, which usually affect poor communities more than richer ones.

In December 2006 the World Bank's annual Global Economic Prospects report trumpeted the prospect of poverty reduction that would be 'nothing short of astounding'.[8] Despite this exciting headline, and the optimistic rates of economic growth predicted, the report goes on to announce that in twenty-five years' time six out of every ten Africans will still be living on under $2 a day.[9] Clearly quite a radical rethink of the relationship between growth and poverty reduction is required if we are to be bolder in our aspirations for the world's poorest people. According to the New Economics Foundation most African countries will require a per capita growth rate between 8–25 per cent to provide as much benefit to the poorest fifth of the population as the redistribution of just 1 per cent of the income of the richest fifth.[10] So often mentioned in the same breath (most notably by the IMF when it named its low-interest lending arm the Poverty Reduction and Growth Facility), growth and poverty reduction can be quite different things. It is unfortunate, given these considerations, that more academic resources are not spent analysing the relationship between aid and poverty reduction, rather than aid and growth. But despite these caveats, since it is a constant refrain of those promoting aid increases that aid will lead to growth, we should look at the evidence.

Methodological problems

Economists love putting together complex models and throwing in all sorts of variants, in order to make generalizations about what has happened in the past and therefore what might happen in the future. While they sometimes reveal interesting information, these models often have intrinsic difficulties. The cross-country methodologies used in modelling for the impact of aid on growth are now regularly criticized. Some countries have seen growth at the same time as receiving aid, others have not. It seems rather ludicrous to add up all the places it has worked and all the places it has not and come up with a global answer. It is not clear what such an answer will teach us. But that is basically what aid and growth economists try to do. What is being tested? If, as I have argued in this book, a salient feature of aid in Africa has been conditionality, aren't we primarily testing whether policies along the lines of the Washington Consensus have led to growth or not, alongside the lesser impacts of the particular financial transfers. The question 'Has aid led to growth?' will then be fundamentally the same question as 'Has a neoliberal economic agenda led to growth?' Meanwhile, the profound institutional impacts of aid are extremely context-specific as well as being cumulative over time, meaning they would not show up in an analysis of growth and contemporaneous aid. Comparing levels of aid with rates of growth over time and across different countries does not take these factors into account.

Most studies have also failed to differentiate between different types of aid. Aid to support health or education systems, or democratic institutions, could only affect growth in the long term, so will not show a positive correlation in the short term. On the other hand, budget and balance of payments support, investments in infrastructure and aid for productive sectors such as agriculture and industry ought in theory to lead to growth in the shorter term.[11] Emergency aid is different again. It will often be negatively correlated with growth simply because it is usually given to countries under severe stress. This might show in models as aid leading to recession because it is hard to separate out cause and effect. So there are a range of technical difficulties. But even if they were methodologically sound, these complex equations, when looked at together, do not paint a coherent picture.

Contradictory evidence

One might sensibly assume that the new surge in aid is based on a consensus among analysts that aid is strongly linked to economic growth. This is the impression given by the various pronouncements of aid proponents in recent years. In fact, despite the profile achieved recently by reports promoting aid as key to growth and development, there is no agreement on this issue. In the 1990s, as Africa continued to get poorer despite many years of aid, it became common in academic circles to say that aid had little or no impact on growth. Meanwhile, its impact on savings and investment was thought to be either neutral or, according to many writers, negative.[12] A survey carried out in 1997 of analyses since the 1970s found exactly that: aid had no significant impact on growth.[13] But this aid pessimism became more nuanced as influential papers were published arguing that aid *could* have a positive impact on growth, but only in countries whose institutions and policies were 'good'.[14] (While you might think this conclusion to be fairly obvious, it was considered at the time to be a major breakthrough.) And, importantly, aid to date had not gone to such countries. Rather than tempering enthusiasm for aid, this finding spurred some to believe that if aid delivery could be improved, aid might lead to growth where previously it had not. This concept proved to be a kind of bridge between the aid pessimism of the 1990s and the renewed aid optimism of today. Selectivity (which means selecting the right countries to give aid to) has since become the buzzword.

There is just as much evidence that aid has an insignificant impact on growth as evidence that its impact is significant, although data suggesting that its impact is negative appear to be in the minority. And the latest evidence and reports (new reports are constantly emerging on this subject) back up both sides of the argument, just as they have in previous aid eras. Two influential reports published shortly after one another present contrasting conclusions. Clemens et al. (November 2004) find that the impact of certain types of aid on growth is very significant and does not depend on the recipient country's policy environment.[15] Meanwhile, Rajan and Subramanian, in a paper called 'Aid and Growth: What Does the Cross-Country Evidence Really Show?' (June 2005), find 'little robust evidence of a positive (or negative) relationship between aid inflows into a country and its economic growth', as well as 'virtually no evidence that aid works better in better policy or institutional or geographical environments, or that certain kinds of aid work better than others'.[16] As one commentator drily notes, 'The diversity of these results suggests that many are fragile.'[17] The consensus that some would like us to think exists on aid and growth is an illusion. Those who claim that aid leads to growth are being selective with the evidence they look at. So are those who say aid does not. Politicians and campaigners who want to push for more aid will enjoy reading Clemens et al. but are unlikely to mention Rajan and Subramanian very much. Nor are they likely to publicize a graph put together by one of aid's leading experts, William Easterly, which shows growth per capita (which is more relevant than growth per se) declining rapidly in Africa as aid hit new levels from the late 1970s onwards.[18]

Macroeconomic impacts

There is one area where it does make sense to look at the impacts of aid transfers per se on economic variables. This is the final set of impacts we should examine: the macroeconomic impacts of aid. When large amounts of foreign money arrive in a country a range of economic impacts are generated that have to be managed by the recipient. While what I have termed direct impacts happen as a direct consequence of the way aid money is spent, and policy impacts are also a direct result of the way conditions are attached to aid, macroeconomic impacts, like aid's harmful impacts on institutions, are not planned. Prices and wages are affected, inflation and exchange rates can rise, and there may be consequences for private savings and investments. These kinds of impacts can be just as important to a person's well-being as the other impacts of aid. When your wage stays the same but the price of food increases you eat less. When your national currency gets stronger against the dollar, your company exports less, and you might lose your job. Macroeconomics matters, not only for that ethereal prize called economic growth, but in the lives of real people.

The main danger for poor people and for a country's overall economic health comes from the way prices change when large amounts of foreign currency enter the country. When the exchange rate is controlled by the central bank such inflows lead to price increases and inflation. Although the IMF's legendary obsession with keeping inflation very low has been unhelpful, it is certainly true that high inflation often hurts the poor – they can buy less with their earnings. This is more of an issue for wage-earners than the rural poor, who are likely to hold most of their savings in real assets (such as livestock) which can often be expected to keep their value as prices rise. Inflation also increases production costs, which reduces competitiveness. It is not just inflation itself but attempts to control it that can have negative consequences if governments restrict access to capital. Increases in aid to Tanzania in the late 1990s led to inflation which in turn led to credit being controlled more tightly, which meant that private firms found it harder to expand.[19]

When the exchange rate is not controlled but is allowed to fluctuate, the impact of large aid inflows is a stronger national currency, which makes exports less competitive and imports cheaper. People depending on export industries and sectors of the economy that compete with imports may well suffer. This is called Dutch Disease, and it should be a concern to African countries receiving aid bonanzas.[20] According to François Bourguignon, the World Bank's chief economist, 'The risks of Dutch Disease appear to be real and potentially serious, particularly when scaling up aid, and heavy aid dependence is likely to extend over many years.'[21] African countries have tended to grow faster when their currencies are weaker, so exchange rate appreciation may slow growth.[22] Even small changes in the exchange rate can have significant effects on exports. The potential effects of scaling aid up in Ethiopia, for example, seem particularly severe. If the exchange rate were to appreciate by 20 per cent, which though large is possible given the substantial new inflows into the country, exports may fall correspondingly from 14 per cent of GDP to 8 per cent by 2015.[23] The consequences for workers in export industries could be severe. The effects of exchange rate appreciation will be less serious in countries that are less dependent on exports.

There are a number of ways to mitigate the harmful effects of Dutch Disease, including taking sensible decisions about how to spend the inflows. If all the foreign currency arriving in a country is spent on imports (to take the extreme case) there should be no effect on the exchange rate or relative prices. Whereas if all the foreign money is spent within the recipient economy (for instance to finance increases in public spending) the effect will be very significant. If inflows are directed at increasing productivity the exchange rate should depreciate, ameliorating the effects of Dutch Disease. An active central bank can also have some success in managing currency appreciations, as the case of Uganda, among other examples, has shown.[24] There are positive outcomes of an appreciating real exchange rate as well. Imports become cheaper, which benefits some consumers and can be especially useful in countries dependent on food imports. The burden of foreign debt should also reduce because you can pay back more dollars with the same amount of national currency. (On the other hand, if exports decrease there will be less foreign money available to pay the debt.)

There are other issues that concern economists, too. Some are worried that high levels of aid dissuade private investors, known as 'crowding out' private investment.[25] Others fear that, because much of the new aid will be spent on social sector employment, wages will rise with knock-on effects throughout the economy, and that skilled workers will leave productive sectors of the economy for activities financed by aid (usually in the social sector), resulting in fewer skilled people actually creating wealth, possibly harming growth.[26] But if aid is spent well it should help an economy to grow. Spending to improve infrastructure like roads and ports should reduce transport and communication costs, thus increasing profits and making the environment more attractive for private investors, reducing fears of crowding out. And spending on social services, quite apart from being the right thing to do for ethical reasons, is also economically sensible. It is vital for a country to have healthy and educated people if its economy is to succeed.

This is a complex area and all the twists and turns of macroeconomic and monetary analysis can be confusing. One could weigh up the range of possible outcomes for a long time but it is worth remembering that economists have been compared to weather forecasters – they are not very good at predicting what is going to happen, but when something has happened they can always explain why (usually in a number of contradictory ways). This brief summary of some of the issues has aimed to demonstrate their importance and the need to take them into account when analysing the overall impact of aid on a country. Are the macroeconomic impacts of large foreign currency inflows likely to cause serious problems for developing countries? Yes. There is consensus across the board that the potentially harmful impacts of large aid increases on exchange rates, prices and inflation, and therefore on exports and growth, and therefore on the livelihoods of ordinary people, should be treated as a very serious concern by recipient countries. Ghana, Mozambique, Tanzania and Uganda all experienced an appreciation of their local currencies when they accessed large amounts of debt relief (which has similar macroeconomic effects as receiving aid) in 2005.[27] Will the negative impacts be possible to manage? Yes, as well.

With promises of significant aid increases to Africa, where aid receipts are already relatively significant, experts are seeking to advise both donors and recipients how best to spend the money and how to ameliorate any potentially damaging macroeconomic impacts. The level of the impact depends on a wide variety of factors, some endogenous (internal to the country's economy) and some exogenous (outside the control of the recipient country). Careful management of aid flows is needed to take potentially harmful effects into account.

Some believe that the changes in wage and price incentives may be so damaging that aid overall will have a negative effect on economic growth.[28] The IMF's intransigent position on inflation has led it again and again to prevent aid spending because of its fear, not unfounded, that the harmful inflationary effects of large aid inflows, especially into social sectors, will undermine the potential good they could do. Others believe that aid's positive impacts will outweigh these negatives, especially as investment in education, health and infrastructure should logically lead to better conditions for poverty reduction.[29] The worst case scenario would probably be that in order to avoid suffering severe macroeconomic impacts, countries choose not to spend the aid they receive, which would mean having to deal with the negative policy and institutional impacts of aid without even benefiting from a productive use of the money. Meanwhile the battle will continue over whether aid, when its macroeconomic impacts are put together with all its other impacts, tends to help or hinder growth. My advice is to take claims by either camp with a substantial pinch of salt.

7 | A better future?

Where are we up to? We have now looked at all four sets of aid's impacts on Africa: direct, policy, institutional and macroeconomic. All are important but seldom are they examined together, and when they are the picture that emerges is murky. While some of the interventions aid has financed over the years have been life-saving or life-changing, others have been detrimental to poor communities and have failed to respect human rights. The policy conditions attached to aid have been harmful and have denied Africa the opportunity to prosper, underpinning decades of stagnation, while the impact the donor–recipient nexus has had on the development of accountable and effective governance in Africa may have contributed to denying a decent chance of democracy to a generation of Africans. Macroeconomic impacts, while manageable, can be severe and must be taken seriously by aid analysts – if they are not they could undermine the good aid increases might do. Many attempts have been made to test aid's overall impact on growth but, taken together, they do not tell a coherent story. There have been far fewer efforts at plotting the overall impact of aid on poverty reduction, let alone on inequality, which can be quite different. Unfortunately, the results of such efforts might not be very positive, given the evidence we have seen in the last four chapters.

In my view, aid has had a series of profound and sometimes unforeseen consequences in Africa that must be acknowledged now if those concerned with Africa's welfare are to respond appropriately. As yet, not enough people are aware of these problems, or have not properly assimilated them into their analyses. This needs to change. When it does I think more people will agree that it is time to begin reducing aid to most countries in Africa, alongside measures to fund development from alternative sources. There is another possibility. Aid optimists do recognize some, though not all, of the problems with aid in the past. An increasing number now accept many of the concerns expressed in this book. The difference is that they believe that things are improving. Their optimism that, somehow, this time will be different is inspiring but misguided, since there is little evidence to suggest that this will be the case. While some aspects of aid giving will improve, the impacts that really matter, the ones linked to policy choices and institutions, are unlikely to do so, and will probably get worse. It is worrying that proponents of aid increases do not appear to want to learn from history. We should now look in more detail at the argument that what Africa will receive in this new era of aid is not only more but also *better* aid.

The 'Paris Agenda'

Since 2005 the phrase 'more and better aid' has become a stalwart of the development lexicon, alongside fair trade and debt cancellation. It is uncommon nowadays to hear the demand for more aid without its sister demand that it also be better. The focus on aid quality as well as quantity is a step forward, to be welcomed. It demonstrates that, at least to a certain extent, the aid community is aware of the faults in the system and is prepared to be self-critical. In 2003 governments and civil society from around the world met in Rome to begin work on some agreed guidelines to improve aid mechanisms. Two years later, in March 2005, the Paris Declaration on Aid Effectiveness was published, encapsulating several 'aid effectiveness' concerns and setting out targets to improve aid in a number of areas. Thirty-five donor countries (including non-OECD countries like Russia and China), twenty-six multilateral agencies and seventy-eight recipient countries have now signed. Underlying the Paris Declaration is the view that 'while the volumes of aid and other development resources must increase to achieve [the Millennium Development Goals], aid effectiveness must increase significantly as well to support partner country efforts to strengthen governance and improve development performance.' But is it plausible that aid to Africa will be transformed in the future, shedding the negative consequences of its past? Is the 'better aid' agenda making a difference?

The Paris Declaration on Aid Effectiveness: five principles[1]

1 Ownership. Developing countries should take the lead in deciding their own policies.
2 Alignment. Donors should support national development strategies, institutions and procedures.
3 Harmonization. Donors should reduce transaction costs for recipient governments by reforming reporting requirements and working better together.
4 Managing for results. Both donors and developing country governments should improve monitoring, decision-making and resource management.
5 Mutual accountability. Donors can hold developing countries to account for their performance but developing country governments should also be able to hold donors to account for whether they have delivered on their commitments.

The Paris Declaration focuses much of its attention on some of the technical aspects of aid giving: how money could be transferred more efficiently; how its (direct) impacts should be monitored; how best to get value for money; how known bottlenecks can be eliminated. These are not unimportant issues. Tying aid to the purchase of goods and services from the donor country makes it between 15–40 per cent less efficient.[2] So, putting pressure on donors to untie aid has to be a good thing, although the official agreed target of 'continued progress over time' cannot really be described as a target, and there is no sign yet that aid is becoming less tied. Bringing down transaction costs would also be positive, if that money could be better spent on other things. Progress on these value-for-money issues would be beneficial for Africa. But while they are central to the official 'better aid' agenda, they have not been emphasized in this book. Why? Because they are tangential to the more serious problems with aid. Even if technicalities such as these improve, the fundamental problems of aid will remain. For all their faults, tied aid and high transaction costs do not essentially harm anyone.

Where does the Paris Declaration stand on the crucially important issues highlighted in this book, like aid's impact on policy choices and on the effectiveness and accountability of state institutions? Review after review of the Paris process, whether by civil society, academia or governments themselves, come up with the same or similar critiques: not ambitious enough, not working fast enough, more problematic than anticipated. A joint statement issued in April 2008 by Afrodad and Eurodad, networks of African and European NGOs specializing in aid and development finance, warns starkly that, 'At the global level, there continues to be little effort to build mechanisms that enhance the overall effectiveness of national institutions, through increased country ownership, operations that raise productivity and yield measurable results in reducing poverty and inequality, and closer coordination with donors and the private sector. In the same vein unreformed supply-driven technical assistance is continuing to favour policy conditionality and undermine ownership.' A detailed Eurodad update on progress under the Paris process makes familiar reading.[3] To those who have been involved in the aid business for some time, it smacks of reports written in previous eras. The same problems are restated, with the same recommendations, side by side with the same occasional stories of change that give hope to campaigners that reform is around the corner. Eurodad strongly criticizes the analysis behind the Paris Declaration, arguing that 'a broad understanding of democracy and development is largely absent in the current aid context' and that 'the Paris Declaration does not take [the accountability of aid downwards from governments to citizens] into account'.

General Budget Support

One significant change in direction in the new era of aid, used by donors to demonstrate progressive reform in the aid system, has been the increase of General Budget Support (GBS, or Direct

Budget Support, DBS). This now accounts for 5 per cent of global aid, with some African governments receiving up to 20–30 per cent of their aid via GBS. The idea is that by providing aid directly to the finance ministry donors can get more of it on budget (thus supporting national procedures) and support the recipient government's broad political direction (rather than picking certain pet projects). By better coordinating their aid they also hope to reduce the resources spent by all parties on administration. Donors have been coordinating their financing efforts so badly that improvements are almost inevitable as this issue becomes more of a priority. Hundreds of different donor-monitoring missions every year are a huge burden on governments with limited human resources and harm the ability of public officials to do their jobs. The Ghanaian Ministry of Health must have better things to do than report to its seventeen different donors in seventeen different ways.[4] According to the World Bank there are more donors per country than ever before, with the average number per country tripling from twelve in the 1960s to thirty-three today. The Tanzanian government, which received 541 donor-monitoring missions in 2006, of which less than a fifth were joint with one or more other donors, actually declares a mission-free period every year so that civil servants can get on with their jobs.[5] Meanwhile the paperwork is immense. There are 35,000 aid transactions a year worldwide, 85 per cent of them worth less than $1m, and most African countries submit around 10,000 quarterly donor reports every year.[6] This suggests that even if significant progress were to be made through the Paris process, it would take a very radical change in direction just to get back to the levels of a few years ago. The move towards GBS is probably a helpful move and the objectives behind it should certainly be applauded. But to date there is little evidence to suggest that the necessary change is under way. According to Eurodad, 'Three years after the Paris Declaration there is no discernible reduction in the burden on recipients of managing multiple aid projects.'[7]

We have seen how the parallel nature of the aid system can undermine the development of a country's systems. But the number of parallel initiatives is growing, not falling, mostly in the health sector. Aid for health has more than doubled since the turn of the millennium to around $15 billion. Most of the funds have gone to new organizations like the GFATM and the US President's Emergency Plan for AIDS Relief (PEPFAR). The structural problem in the aid business is that while new aid machinery is being created all the time, the older organizations tend not to disappear, leading to an ever more complex landscape. The United Nations Development Programme (UNDP) calculates that there are now more than 1,000 financing mechanisms operating at a global level.[8] Donor activities have tripled since the mid-1990s from around 20,000 in 1997 to nearer 60,000 in 2004, while their average size has been cut from over $2.5 million to a little over $1.5 million eight years later.[9] According to most reviews, the problems with technical assistance are not getting solved, and the predictability of aid is not generally improving either (with some exceptions), making it hard for recipient governments to plan ahead.[10]

While it may seem obvious that donors should sit down and coordinate their aid giving, such coordination might be entrenching and continuing the system of consolidated donor pressure that has done such damage to Africa's chances of development. According to the Reality of Aid Network, 'Many of the reforms suggested by the Paris Declaration on their own may in fact further undermine [the ability of poor people to claim their] rights and the promotion of democratic processes, the rule of law, and parliamentary processes.'[11] Harmonization and coordination can be a double-edged sword in the aid business. While less bureaucracy means more time available to do more important things, variety among donors can sometimes be a good thing if it allows innovation and even competition, whereby recipients might refuse some offers of aid and accept others, depending on the modalities. Harmonization of conditions is quite different from harmonizing procedures. In one sense aid to Africa has been well harmonized for some time. The biggest donors have lined up behind decisions made by the IMF and World Bank about who should and should not receive funds. If they had not, and had broken ranks more often, the immense pressure to reform, led by IFI aid conditionalities, would have been considerably diluted. A civil society statement signed by hundreds of organizations representing seventy-nine countries expresses concern that far from making progress on reducing conditions, new aid modalities are leading to 'broader and deeper' conditions, which continue to harm the interests of poor and marginalized communities: 'Donor harmonization has the potential to reduce rather than increase policy space for recipients if it means that all donors make their aid conditional on the policy reforms demanded by the World Bank and IMF in particular.'[12] Donors are working in coalitions to draw up complex agreements with recipient countries that include a large number of conditions covering policies, processes and outcomes. For instance, Tanzania's Performance Assessment Framework (PAF), which is attached to its Budget Support Agreement, has a twelve-page matrix of conditions, and forty-nine pages recounting the government's progress or lack thereof on the conditions.[13] Because the PAF brings together the conditions of all the donors, it is hard to change it once it is prepared. IMF macroeconomic conditions are still the basis of official aid, programme-based or otherwise. Often sold as simply a sensible part of aid management, these IMF conditions are political and highly controversial. The first indicator of Malawi's PAF is to be on track with its IMF-monitored macroeconomic programme, meaning that all the conditions of the IMF programme are simply cobbled together as one indicator.

The same old ways of bypassing the legitimate decision-making bodies appear to be in evidence again, with donors setting up a range of working groups to work with government officials on policy formulation. While apparently seeking to strengthen the capacity and legitimacy of government ministries, a new layer of policymaking is being introduced, where the role of legitimate political and social institutions remains unclear at best. Those horror stories about country development plans being written in Washington and faxed to the relevant country government for approval are not a thing of the past. Sierra Leone's PAF (late 2006) was drafted by donors before being presented to the government, which can negotiate the timing but not the substance of the conditions. The parliament, let alone civil society, does not see the final draft.[14] Niger's second PRSP (early 2007) was drafted in Washington by representatives of the Niger government and World Bank, UNDP, the EC, Belgian and IMF officials. The UNDP then paid for a foreign consultant to finalize the strategy before it was presented to the parliament, not for amendments or even approval, but for information. And the final irony is that the indicator used in the Paris Declaration to assess the presence or otherwise of a good quality and operational national development strategy will be monitored by none other than the World Bank. According to Eurodad, the general trend is for budget support to 'come hand in hand with more intrusion by donors in government policy making through ever more detailed matrices of policy conditions and performance indicators'.[15]

There are always enough examples of stilted progress to give hope that times are changing for the better, provided the evidence is used selectively. There has been a reduction in the number of conditions linked to budget support in Mozambique and Ghana, for example.[16] GBS allows more aid to be spent on recurrent costs (such as wages and other inputs) and evidence from Ghana suggests that transferring money this way was more predictable and efficient than other ways of doing it.[17] Other studies argue that transaction costs actually rise.[18] While limited efforts to increase ownership are likely to have some positive effects, as the problem is better understood now than previously, it is hard to see how the fundamental problem will go away as long as large amounts of money are received from external players. Attempts to make aid processes 'mutually accountable' are unlikely to succeed because the profound power imbalances between donor and recipient are intrinsic and cannot be surgically removed by better management. According to one Niger government official, 'These negotiations are *by their nature* unequal as we need the money.'[19]

New era, same problems

Why has there been so little progress on the policy and institutional problems of aid, despite the constant pledges to change? Some governments and institutions appear genuinely to want to allow more decision-making autonomy in aid-recipient countries. The UK government promised in 2005 to 'not make our aid conditional on specific policy decisions by partner governments or attempt to impose policy choices on them (including in sensitive economic areas such as privatisation or trade liberalization)',[20] although it added that it will still follow IMF guidelines on macroeconomic management, which undermines an otherwise laudable sentiment. A handful of other countries have moved in this direction, including Norway, which in December 2007 announced that it was withholding 25 per cent of its planned increase in financing to the World Bank because it was 'not completely satisfied with the progress the World Bank has made in living up to its principles on conditionality'.

But most donors do not seem to think there is a problem. Many who have supported changes in conditionality processes have done so not because they disagree with the content of the conditions, but because they recognize that the way conditions have been imposed has sometimes not been effective in achieving policy change. They want reform but have found it hard to buy with aid money. So they are looking at other options, like selectivity. Those arguing for selectivity say that it only makes sense to give aid to countries which already have 'good policies'. In a speech to the Monterrey Conference on Financing for Development in 2002 George Bush appeared not to have read the script: 'Money that is not accompanied by legal and economic reform is oftentimes wasted ... Sound economic policies unleash the enterprise and creativity necessary for development. So we will reward nations that have more open markets and sustainable budget policies, nations where people can start and operate a small business without running the gauntlets of bureaucracy and bribery.'[21] Three years later the head of USAID was equally explicit, confirming that 'we have also taken steps to ensure that development assistance funds go to countries that have proved their commitment to change'. Selectivity, rather than out-and-out conditionality, is the basis of much aid giving in the new era, most notably that of the US's Millennium Challenge Account (MCA) which uses seventeen country performance indicators to guide aid decisions.[22] The World Bank judges countries according to its Country Policy and Institutional Assessment (CPIA) and allocates more money to countries with higher marks. Both the MCA and the CPIA have their own ideas about what constitutes good and bad policies and therefore what should be rewarded with aid money. You can probably guess what they are. Mozambique's CPIA score in 2002 was only average because of IFI concerns about its tariffs on sugar and cashew nuts. It got less money from the World Bank that year.[23]

Donors say they are trying to reduce conditions. But far from separating itself from economic policy considerations, aid 'is becoming more selective and focused on countries that demonstrate capacity and stronger performance', according to the World Bank's chief economist François Bourguignon, who finds that the 'selectivity of aid according to country policies is especially strong among low-income countries'.[24] One suspects that the United States and other countries sign the now traditional and more or less annual recommitments to recipient country ownership over policies more because of peer and campaigner pressure than because they really agree. Even apparently progressive governments are equivocal on the issue. Gordon Brown, the British Prime Minister, promises 'tough conditionality' attached to aid to ensure that recipients 'pursue stable, equitable and sustainable economic growth, and agree to international monitoring of their poverty reduction plans'.[25] Selectivity is a more subtle way of pressurizing governments to implement certain policies, only this time they need to implement them in advance of receiving aid, rather than during the period of aid disbursement. As explicit conditions continue to receive criticism, other tactics may come to the fore, but the fundamental pressure on African countries to adopt certain policies in order to access financing remains.

The seventy-nine-country civil society statement states that the Paris process 'largely ignores' the issue of conditionality.[26] But policy conditionality is not so much ignored as not taken seriously enough. The usual donor intentions to respond to national processes and support policy plans drawn up by recipient governments are restated. Again. But there is little or no recognition of the fundamental problems elaborated in this book. Reading through the seminal texts of this aid era, the reports of the Africa Commission and the UN Millennium Project, it becomes clear why. Apart from making the usual pat remarks about reducing 'excessive' conditionality there is no serious discussion of the issue. What about the other major issue, aid's negative impact on the development of democracy and effective and accountable institutions? Again, there is no recognition of this issue in the analyses that form the basis of the Paris Declaration. The Africa Commission calls for a doubling of aid to improve capacity and promote accountability, rightly locating weakness in these two key areas at the heart of Africa's troubles. It urges donors to help broaden participation in government processes, strengthen institutions and build accountable budgetary processes. The IFIs and donors should 'support and not undermine institutions of accountability in African countries, for example by helping countries to strengthen international codes and standards and by avoiding heavy burdens of reporting'. At no stage, however, does it wrestle with the central paradox of aid – that the act of aid giving in itself undermines both state capacity and accountability. The report of the UN Millennium Project also fails to look at this subject. Given the overwhelming importance being placed on governance by donors in this new era of aid, it might seem incomprehensible that they would not take seriously the grave concerns about the harmful effects of aid on institutions. Yet sometimes it appears that decision-makers and their advisers have simply not talked to African experts about these issues, let alone read the substantial literature on the subject. Did the authors not know of these problems, or were the problems simply too inconvenient to acknowledge? Either way, with such an incomplete analysis of the present situation, is it likely that effective recommendations will emerge? These are complicated problems, but they will not disappear simply by denying their existence.

Unfortunately, concerns about these issues will worsen as aid increases. Large-scale aid to Europe after the Second World War lasted only a few years and never exceeded 3 per cent of GDP for any one country.[27] Korea and Taiwan received substantial aid but only for a decade or so.[28] In contrast, aid to Africa has become the defining element of a number of African economies, and a vital component in most. Africa receives over 9 per cent of its GDP in aid and many countries receive much more than that. Most are now in their third or even fourth decade of large-scale aid receipts.[29] Two leading economists project that, if the current targets are met, twenty-seven of Africa's thirty-eight low income countries are likely to receive aid inflows equivalent to over 50 per cent of total public expenditure by 2015, while for twelve that figure will be 75 per cent. That compares with seventeen and nine at present. In this expected scenario, Burkina Faso, Madagascar and Mali, for example, will see ODA grow from less than 50 per cent of the budget to more than 65 per cent. Uganda, which currently receives aid equivalent to 64 per cent of its government expenditure, would see that level rise to 79 per cent, while Tanzania would see the ratio increase from 77 per cent to 87 per cent.[30] This means almost total dependence. The fundamental problem that governments will be more accountable to donors than their own citizens is set to worsen, despite the best efforts of the aid community.

Less and better aid

What about the other two sets of impacts, macroeconomic and direct? The potential for problems at a macroeconomic level will increase as aid to Africa rises. However, that does not mean problems are inevitable. We can be reasonably optimistic that with so much written on the subject recipient countries will take appropriate measures to minimize potential costs associated with price changes and other unplanned impacts. It is hard to say whether the direct impacts of aid will improve. There is no evidence to suggest that fewer controversial aid projects are under way than in previous eras. Lessons learned over the years have led to much greater emphasis being placed on consultations with people potentially affected by big aid projects before they go ahead. African civil society is relatively weak when compared with Latin America and Asia, so strengthening civil society both financially and politically would be a good use of some of the funds saved from reducing aid to governments. Organizations and movements that monitor people in power, whether in government or in the private sector, are the foundation stones of a society in which human rights are respected and the needs of the most excluded taken into account.

Sometimes it seems that almost everyone in the aid industry (especially those coming to the end of many years of service) has their own shopping list of changes that would make the aid system better. Some suggest technical improvements that will have little impact on the substantial problems described in this book. Others call for more radical changes. Rather than add to the shopping list I prefer to re-emphasize my first principle, and one of the key messages of this book: aid should be better evaluated. This will lead to better decisions in future aid giving. If we are going to take bold decisions rather than safe ones, this becomes all the more important. The Paris Declaration includes a section on monitoring aid's impacts, which is a step forward. But it is not enough just to keep monitoring aid's quantifiable impacts, direct and macroeconomic. All the impacts of aid, positive and harmful, long and short term, easy to quantify and hard to enumerate, must be taken into account, however complex that exercise might be, if we are to get a true picture of how aid is contributing to or undermining efforts to reduce poverty. Aid givers, from northern governments to small NGOs, have intervened politically as well as humanely and need to recognize the overall impacts of that intervention.

Given all the problems already being caused by excessive aid monitoring missions, it would be foolhardy to call for *more* monitoring. Rather, we need *better* monitoring, and a better understanding of aid's complex impacts to underpin a more rigorous methodology. These analyses must be independent. There are obvious incentives around in the aid business – for instance, most people writing about it make a living from it. I believe that if and when a 'net' analysis of aid's impacts is carried out by independent experts, the central tenet of this book will be supported – that while aid does some good, it also does harm, and overall there are much more important ways for rich countries to support development in Africa. Each recipient country will present different results, with some African countries perhaps being able to use more aid. Most will benefit from a reduction in the amount of aid they receive, along with an increase in alternative sources of funds for poverty reduction.

The rich world has been giving aid to the poor world for roughly half a century. It is a sensible assumption that during that time mistakes have been made, as well as progress, and that lessons have been learnt about what and what not to do. African and donor country civil society and responsible governments alike have spent a great deal of effort to ensure that the mistakes of the past do not occur in the new era. The hard work of all those trying to make aid do more good and less harm is important. We need to continue to fight negative tendencies in the aid system. But present attempts to improve 'aid effectiveness' do not begin to deal with the deep problems of states dependent on aid, and approach the problem of aid conditionality only at a superficial level. Donor governments have a habit of promising reform but delivering only cosmetic change. Recipient governments are often more interested in the quantity of money they receive than the quality of its impacts. It is naïve to expect aid to look substantially different in ten years' time from how it looks today. This is in part because the political and economic incentives to use aid to benefit donor countries are as strong as ever, as we will see in the next chapter. Rather than focusing on more aid, and calling for better aid as a second-tier goal, which is what campaigners have done up till now, it is time to change course. Africa needs less and better aid.

8 | Why is aid really going up?

Why has the aid pessimism of the 1990s turned to the aid optimism of the new millennium? The evidence discussed so far is at best inconclusive regarding the impact of aid on long-term poverty reduction in poor countries. At worst, the probability that aid undermines the development of accountable institutions is high, while the negative consequences of policy conditionalities in Africa have almost certainly outweighed the positive effects of some of the important aid spending that has taken place. There appears little reason to believe that the harmful impacts of the past will somehow evaporate in this new era of aid. With evidence as mixed as this, what can explain the renewed enthusiasm for aid among the development community? The answer is that political considerations are driving the new era of aid more than evidence.

Rajan and Subramanian, the two leading IMF economists we met briefly in Chapter 6, have written that 'the literature [on the relationship between aid and growth] has sometimes followed a cycle in which one paper finds a result, and is followed by another paper with a twist, either overturning or qualifying the previous result, followed by another, and so on. This has had some undesirable effects on policy with advocates selectively using results to bolster their preferred view on aid.'[1] This is precisely what is happening in the new era of aid, not only with the aid and growth literature, but with all the evidence associated with aid. What we are seeing more closely resembles policy-based evidence than evidence-based policy. Increases in aid and the associated aid optimism are functions of political strategy and expediency, and much of the evidence, as we have seen, is simply ignored or wished away.

A good anecdotal example of how evidence can follow the

current political context is the very way Rajan and Subramanian, in the same paper, choose to present their conclusion that there is 'no robust evidence' of a link between aid and growth: '[The findings], which relate to the past, do not imply that aid cannot be beneficial in the future. But they do suggest that for aid to be effective in the future, the aid apparatus will have to be rethought. ... Thus, our findings support efforts under way at national and international levels to understand and improve aid effectiveness.'[2] That is certainly a fair conclusion. But one cannot help wondering whether they might have said something different if they had been presenting precisely the same data, but in the mid-1990s. Then, they might well have concluded that their data supported the aid pessimism of the time. Today, however, they interpret their results in the light of a new context of aid optimism and are wary of bucking the orthodox trend. Bill Easterly, one of the foremost experts on aid, tells the fascinating story of how a paper linking aid to growth in good policy environments (Craig Burnside and David Dollar's seminal 'Aid, Policies, and Growth', first published in 1997) became the basis of donor policy, not because it was more sound academically than other investigations (Easterly strongly questions its conclusions) but because it was exactly the message donors wanted to hear in the new era of aid.

The big difference between this era of aid to Africa and previous eras is profound aid dependency. But there is another difference as well. For the first time there is compelling evidence (some of which I have presented in this book) to show that aid has, at best, very mixed results and, at worst, can hinder economic and political progress. Whereas in the past the decision to give aid may well have been a sensible response to dire need, now, with the evidence casting serious doubt on the value of aid in the fight against poverty and inequality, and with a range of more effective ways to help, it is unacceptable to continue down a misguided course. When the evidence changes, as Keynes famously asserted, we should change our minds. The question is not why rich countries are giving aid, but why they are *still* giving aid. So far in this book we have given donors the benefit of the doubt in assuming that their reasons for giving aid are enlightened and humanitarian. But foreign affairs introduce more complicated motives; there are other, less altruistic, forces at play. There are two main reasons for the donor focus on aid. First, aid is the easiest and least costly way for politicians to be seen to be responding to the continuing and unacceptable poverty that exists in most of the world, particularly in Africa. And second, far from being costly, aid is a cost-efficient way of buying economic advantage and political support.

Aid is easy

While rich countries have become significantly richer since the 1980s or so, Africa has become poorer, while Latin America has stagnated. Asian countries, particularly India and China, which account for a third of the world's population, have seen impressive growth, but there is mixed evidence regarding its poverty-reducing impacts.[3] Globally, the average income in the richest twenty countries in the world is thirty-seven times that in the poorest twenty.[4] As poverty overseas becomes ever more visible through improving media communications, Western politicians appear to have discovered a renewed determination to do something about it. Some are driven by passionate concern, most obviously perhaps the UK's Prime Minister, Gordon Brown, who has spent a great deal of personal effort and political capital pushing through international commitments on aid and debt. In a few countries international poverty has become an election issue, giving a further reason for politicians to engage. The 2005 Make Poverty History campaigns in the United Kingdom and elsewhere, which called for more and better aid, debt cancellation and fairer trade rules, brought public pressure to bear on politicians to act in response to poverty. The commitments of the European governments to reach the 0.7 per cent target by 2015 are clearly linked to this pressure. There is a bipartisan consensus in an otherwise divided United States Congress on more aid to Africa. For both Democrats and Republicans, aid is an act of faith.

During his presidency George W. Bush responded particularly to a right-wing Christian block which supports aid increases, especially on AIDS. Other countries, where public campaigns are not large enough to constitute a serious electoral constituency, have been pressured into action by the proactive efforts of their peers. Thus Japan responded to bold statements from EU governments and to the huge Live 8 concerts with public announcements of aid increases in 2005 (yet to be fulfilled). Some governments give aid in part to appease those constituencies, at home and abroad, that are disillusioned with other aspects of foreign policy, most notably the UK and US governments, whose credibility has been seriously undermined by the Iraq war.

But even development experts who support more aid would probably put it low down the list of actions Northern governments should take if they *really* wanted to help poor countries.[5] Why is aid the focus of rich country action when its impact on growth and development in the long term is so questionable? The answer is quite simple. Initiatives that would have a much more significant impact on poverty also have a higher cost to donors. The cost of aid is almost irrelevant to rich countries, ranging from between 0.1–0.2 per cent (the United States and Japan) and just under 1 per cent (some small European countries) of GNI. Double aid and the economies of Germany, or the United States, or France, hardly blink. Business lobby groups, trade unions and other powerful interests in rich countries are not concerned about aid, since it costs them nothing, but they get very involved when issues of trade and the role of the private sector are raised. Real solutions do affect them. Even though the long-term gains for everyone from reducing poverty are clear, there may well be a short-term political or financial cost to certain sectors if poverty-reducing policies are introduced. The West is giving aid not because it works, but because it is easy. It is the path of least resistance, regardless of its effectiveness. It pleases the general public because it looks generous and it buys time with campaigners who walk away frustrated that their demands for structural change have again been ignored, but partly satisfied that at least more aid was promised. By focusing efforts on increasing aid, Western politicians are able to avoid ceding ground on more difficult issues, such as trade and other issues from which rich countries continue to draw massive benefits under the current system.

Aid buys friends

This brings us to the second fundamental reason for aid's popularity: far from being costly, aid actually delivers a range of benefits to donors. In 1962 US President John Kennedy asserted that 'Aid is a method by which the United States maintains a position of influence and control around the world. ... Really I put it right at the top of the essential programs in protecting the security of the free world.'[6] It is widely accepted that throughout the Cold War aid was given to countries by both East and West in order to buy their support, often without regard for the possibly harmful impacts of such aid. It is taken as read that aid fell during the 1990s as a consequence of the fall of the Soviet Union and the end of the Cold War. Clearly, donor choices about aid spending were not governed by an analysis of poverty in Africa, which was increasing exponentially in the 1990s, but by geopolitical considerations quite separate from moral duty. Now, in the post 9/11 global context, donor countries again want to use aid to influence the politics of other countries. Historically, aid has tended not to be given to those countries most in need of money, nor even to those with what donors regard as 'good policy environments'.[7] The largest recipients of US aid, to take the world's biggest donor and pre-eminent superpower, are not the poorest countries but those the United States sees as strategically important. Countries like Israel, Jordan, Georgia and Armenia topped the list in 2006.[8] There is evidence to suggest that the World Bank and IMF have followed US strategic priorities – the United States is the largest shareholder of both institutions.[9]

The effects of the War on Terror are being felt in Africa. Following the 9/11 terror strikes US aid money poured into the Horn of Africa, which is considered a major source of terrorism.

According to the data available to the public, Eritrea received almost three times as much aid from the United States in the period 2001–2005 ($113 million) as in the five years beforehand. Along with its rival, Ethiopia, also vying for US support in the border dispute, it was one of only four African countries to back the Iraq war. Aid came to an abrupt end in 2006, as the United States began to contemplate putting Eritrea on its list of state sponsors of terrorism (which also means no more money from the IMF and World Bank). Djibouti (where there is a US–French military base) has seen aid increase from $10 million in the five years before 2001 to almost $60 million afterwards.[10] These figures do not include military aid, which also skyrocketed. What is driving US decisions about aid giving to these extremely poor countries? Is it poverty reduction? Is it democracy, human rights and the rule of law? Or does it have more to do with 'homeland security'? Haven't we seen this before?

In February 2003, when the United States and the United Kingdom were desperately trying to cobble together the votes they needed in the UN Security Council to legitimize their planned war on Iraq, they targeted Angola, Cameroon and Guinea, which were serving on the Council, Guinea as president. Despite overwhelming opposition to the war throughout Africa, these and other countries were aware of the financial costs a vote against the war might have. According to Ismael Gaspar Martins, Angola's Ambassador to the United Nations, 'For a long time now, we have been asking for help to rebuild our country after years of war. No one is tying the request to support on Iraq but it is all happening at the same time.'[11] It is no coincidence that Baroness Amos, Tony Blair's special envoy to Africa, arrived in Guinea just hours after the key resolution on Iraq was tabled at the UN. In these situations countries remember what happened to Yemen when it voted against authorizing the first Gulf War in 1991. The Secretary of State at the time, James Baker, warned that it could be 'the most expensive vote in history' before cutting US aid to one of the world's poorest countries by 82 per cent.[12] Plenty of other tools are used to gain political leverage, trade preferences being the most obvious, but aid is a significant one. The most recent of the many studies demonstrating a statistical correlation between foreign aid and voting patterns on the UN Security Council implies that US aid buys UN Security Council votes (although the aid of other donors appears not to),[13] while another analysis shows US aid rising by an average of 59 per cent when countries have a seat on the Security Council.[14]

In the new era of aid a small number of donors, especially in Europe, have focused their aid increasingly on the poorest countries and have sought to pursue aid financing in isolation from other foreign policy interests. In so far as aid is seen to serve the national interest it is the enlightened and long-term national interest of building strong and wealthy trading partners and reducing the threat of failed states.[15] The UK government appears so far to have resisted the temptation to drop its exclusive poverty focus. At one stage it considered introducing a policy whereby aid money would be given to countries on the condition that they take back asylum seekers, but it eventually decided against this and has made clear that security and other considerations remain secondary to poverty reduction aims in aid spending.[16] These shifts have led some to believe that the new era of aid heralds not only more money but also a fundamentally different approach to how aid should be spent. But this new focus remains the exception, not the rule. Most aid departments still sit within foreign affairs ministries and there are strong indications that any movement towards seeing aid as separate from foreign policy objectives is not shared by the United States, which accounts for almost a quarter of OECD aid. In a speech to British parliamentarians in 2005 Andrew Natsios, then head of USAID, explicitly rejected what he described as the 'European' approach. It is a lucid analysis, worth quoting at length.

> The European debate addresses the development challenge largely devoid of foreign policy or national security considerations. It is doubtful for how much longer this posture can be maintained before overriding security concerns impinge on the

debate ... 'Pure' development, that is, development abstracted from foreign policy concerns in the real world and the challenges they present, is not likely to be sustainable over the long term, I fear. The history of more than half a century of foreign assistance in the US demonstrates this ...

I believe that the principal reason for the decline of official development assistance and the institutional damage to USAID in the 1990s was the absence of a clearly understood foreign threat to western interests which foreign aid could remedy. I am dealing with the legacy of the 1990s at the dawn of a new century, a time of global terror and a renewed emphasis on development. It is a moment of historic realignment in the national security structure of the federal government, including USAID, where changes have been dramatic, both in funding levels and in internal restructuring ...

During the Cold War, the dynamics of a bipolar world and competition with the Soviet Union required us to guard and expand our alliance systems. Diplomatically, this meant friendship with some unsavoury leaders and regimes ... Our foreign assistance programming ... was built around stability, not transformative development. Today this has changed. We now realise that civilised life depends crucially on transforming the troubled regions of the world. Unlike the Cold War, we are now menaced more by 'fragile states than by conquering states' ... Opening up the developing world to economic opportunity and expanding the ranks of democratic states are now vital to our own national security. These are the goals of what future generations might call the Bush Doctrine, and they are now central to the mission of USAID.[17]

Natsios predicts that the changes to USAID as a result of this understanding of the role of aid will be sustained for some time to come. Thus, while some countries are seeking to separate aid from foreign policy aims, the United States explicitly, and many others more subtly, are moving in quite the opposite direction. His hope that foreign assistance will be more concerned with 'transformative development' than previous concerns with 'stability' has some merit, but we should probably take this 'realization' with a dose of scepticism. US short- to medium-term interests are still that countries should be stable enough to reduce potential threats, rather than transformed enough to reduce poverty. Recent large increases in US aid to West Africa, where France has always been a dominant foreign power, are strongly linked to the fact that the United States has identified the region as the potential source of a quarter of its energy needs in fifteen years' time.[18] It will need allies and a certain amount of stability to achieve this goal, but not necessarily much poverty reduction or respect for human rights. The US military's new Africa Command, AFRICOM, will operate from Liberia and will, according to President Bush, 'enhance our efforts to bring peace and security to the people of Africa and promote our common goals of development, health, education, democracy, and economic growth in Africa'.[19]

Aid is a good investment

As well as seeking to buy friends in the world of international relations, donors use aid to buy commercial benefits, either directly buying preferential treatment for companies based in donor countries, using tied aid to benefit domestic companies and industries, or influencing recipient country policy with aid conditions so as to make trade rules and the investment climate more suitable for these companies. Donors have tended to be quite explicit about the link between aid and economic interests. In 1980 the UK's Minister for Overseas Development announced that the new Conservative government would 'give greater weight in the allocation of our aid to political, industrial and commercial objectives alongside our basic developmental objectives'.[20] The UK government changed tack on this issue when, in 1997, the incoming Labour government created a separate Department for International Development, breaking it away from the Foreign Office. UK aid is no longer tied to the purchase of UK goods and services, and must by law be entirely focused on poverty reduction. But most donors, including new donors such as China which are playing an increasingly important role in aid financing, appear to see giving aid as part of promoting their commercial interests in other countries, just as traditional donors always have. China's rapid growth and consequent need for vast amounts of raw materials is clearly and unashamedly behind its new interest in giving aid to Africa – it has very quickly become one of the continent's largest donors, and has already been influencing African politics. The Chinese ambassador to Zambia threatened to cut ties with the country should an opposition candidate that had criticized Chinese investment practices in the country be elected in the 2006 presidential elections.[21] In January 2008, China shipped 5,000 tons of food aid to Zimbabwe.[22] While it is obvious to Western analysts that this kind of aid is part of a political process aimed at benefiting Chinese trade and investment, when Western donors give aid, somehow only altruistic reasons get press coverage. Even India is giving aid to Africa. In a summit with fourteen African countries in April 2008, India announced that it would give $500 million in grants over the next five years and double its credit to $5.4 billion.[23] With 400 million poor people of its own to attend to, this largesse is obviously not about poverty reduction. It is intended to buy economic benefits (particularly in the light of India's growing energy requirements) and political support – the African Union bloc of fifty-three countries will come in handy as India continues its bid for a permanent seat on the UN Security Council.

Meanwhile, 58 per cent of aid is tied to the purchase of goods and services from the donor country.[24] Italy is one of the worst offenders, tying over 70 per cent of its aid, although this is down from 92 per cent in 2001.[25] The Italian government has spent more than $150 million on the Bumbuna hydroelectric dam project in Sierra Leone which started in the 1970s. Luckily, the contractors are Italian (a company called Salcost) so the Italian economy will not have lost out very much. A more recent example is the multi-million-dollar contract to update Angola's telecommunications network, paid for with Italian aid money and awarded to Italian multinational Alcatel.[26] CARE International recently refused to administer about $45 million worth of US food aid on the grounds that it is little more than a subsidy for American farmers, which hurts rather than helps farmers in Africa,[27] not to mention the scandalous attempt to introduce controversial genetically modified products into Zambia as emergency food aid.[28]

You do not have to be a conspiracy theorist to realize that the conditions attached to aid are motivated in part by what donors feel to be in their own interests. The role of the international financial institutions has always been highly politicized, as the major shareholders are the developed countries. It is hard to mask the political colour of an organization like the World Bank, which has replaced the relatively neutral James Wolfensohn as its president first by Paul Wolfowitz, one of the architects of neo-conservatism in the Bush administration, and then by Robert Zoellick, the former US Trade Secretary, infamous for his single-minded pursuit of US interests in the WTO and other trade negotiations. The general dismantling of protectionism in other countries is the great project of the rich world, and while multilateral negotiations have been conducted at the WTO (or its predecessors), the use of aid conditions has been a crucial weapon in the armoury. Liberalization has led to far greater possibilities for developed country businesses in the developing world, and this trend is continuing apace. A recent report on reforms in government procurement linked to donor conditionality finds that 'It is not clear if they are succeeding in bringing about effective change in [improving governance]. They are, however, most definitely succeeding in promoting procurement systems that increase opportunities for foreign firms.'[29] A new concept, known as 'aid-for-trade', is promoting the substitution of trade taxes with aid. In an interview with US President George Bush, Bob Geldof, an influential aid activist, responds to the president's concerns about high tariffs disrupting trade in Africa by reminding him of the importance of the income derived by cross-border tariffs. Sadly, rather than arguing for the right of African countries to apply the tariffs they see fit to balance trade openness, protecting domestic enterprise and fiscal requirements, Geldof then suggests that aid would be a useful replacement: 'You have to help take them down. Aid for trade.'[30] Given the evidence presented in this book, this can be said to be generally the wrong thing to do. No wonder so many Africans see aid as little more than bribery on a grand scale.

Aid is thus an extremely sensible investment on the part of rich countries, for both geopolitical and economic reasons. Donors have played a leading role in creating the aid dependency, which they now profess to be concerned by, and it is not an exaggeration to say that, in terms of *realpolitik*, it does them no harm to keep it that way. Moreover, the short-term costs of policies that would really help Africa are higher. African countries should be given immediate and unconditional access to rich country markets, but should have the right to restrict imports and foreign investment in their own. Although in the long term a richer Africa will be a healthier trading partner to the benefit of everyone, in the short term that could be a lose-lose recipe for Western companies.

Recipient governments

With all these reasons for continuing to give aid, it is not hard to understand why donors continue to ignore the evidence and promote aid rather than other policies that would do more to help reduce poverty. But why do African governments continue to accept it? The answer is indeed the obvious one. Recipient governments have strong incentives to maintain the aid giving process because they are in desperate economic straits and need all the help they can get. It is not clear, for many recipients, how they would fill a 'financing gap' left by the removal of aid and, conversely, it is usually quite obvious to governments how they might spend more free money should it come their way. No country *wants* to take aid and all that goes with it. But in the short term, aid is the easiest way to fill the resource gap, and it strengthens the hand of governments and the individuals within them. The fact that in the long term it creates dependency in

Africa and undermines attempts finally to find a path out of poverty is too theoretical a consideration for many governments given their short-term need. The cases of African countries refusing aid are few.

The same is not true throughout the world. On other continents there is a backlash against aid and the conditions that come with it. It is not easy to refuse cheap money, but many developing country governments have simply had enough of the negative impacts of the aid relationship on their countries and people. The fierce anti-IMF rhetoric in South America and elsewhere indicates that a sizeable proportion of people consider the IMF to be largely responsible for the failed policies adopted in their countries over the last few years. In Argentina the newly elected president, Cristina Kirchner, promised not just to reform her country's relationship with the IMF, but to ensure that the next generation would never even have to hear of the organization![31] Like Argentina, Brazil has paid off vast debts to the IMF in order to free itself from IMF pressure, while Bolivia is unlikely to sign another agreement with the IMF now that its debts to the institution have been cancelled.[32] Despite the relatively good price of IMF loans compared with the market, these countries prefer not to be in debt to the IMF because of the pressure they then fall under to enact policies which they would prefer not to. Across the world those countries that are able to are building up substantial financial reserves, partly because they do not want to go to the IMF for financial assistance if they fall into problems in the future. India's recent dismissal of all but the largest donor programmes, though from a lower income level, also illustrates the trade-off between political costs and financial benefits.[33] Importantly, all these countries, apart from Bolivia, which is now receiving financial support from other countries in the region, have in common the fact that they are not aid dependent – otherwise they would be unlikely to be so brave. If African countries were not so dependent on donor-financing there is no doubt they would be doing the same thing. They need to begin the process of reducing aid dependency, rather than stoking calls for even more aid. But they can only do so if there is also change at the global level as well.

Campaigners

So much for the incentives of both donors and recipients to increase aid. International organizations such as the World Bank, IMF and UN agencies respond to their members, who are either donors or recipients, and most depend directly on aid money for their survival, so it is easy to see why they come out in support of aid as well. What still remains unclear is why pressure groups and apparently independent analysts have for so long championed the cause of more government-to-government aid in the face of the mounting evidence. The job of campaigning groups, so often effective in influencing government policy, is to work out what needs to be done and campaign to achieve it. Since the 1990s the international campaigns on trade have been loud and clear, based on sound research. Climate change is moving up the agenda of campaigning groups. But aid has always been the top advocacy priority for almost all international charities. In the United States, the ONE campaign is gathering pace, led by U2's frontman Bono and supported by the major development agencies. Its banner call, drowning out its other demands, is for the United States to raise its foreign aid to 1 per cent of government expenditure. The biggest campaign in UK history, the Make Poverty History campaign of 2005, campaigned on three issues – aid, debt and trade – but by the time Live 8 made the campaign truly global, it was clear what the major call was: more money. The campaign fizzled out when it moved to the thornier issues of trade and aid effectiveness. The way this campaign evolved offers insights into how calls for more aid invariably trump demands for change that would really help Africa.

In the summer of 2004 leading UK charities sat down together to draw up a list of demands for the UK government in what they hoped would be one of the biggest public campaigns the United Kingdom had ever seen. They were right. Make Poverty History 2005 was massive, even before Bob Geldof's Live 8 took it to another level and to an even wider audience. Its international partner, the Global Call to Action Against Poverty, enlisted the support of 40 million people in thirty-six countries.[34] The Make Poverty History coalition eventually encompassed hundreds of organizations and community groups, but at its core remained the big international charities. Some within the coalition initially wanted the campaign to focus exclusively on aid – it was just going to be called the 'double aid' campaign – but they finally agreed that aid, debt and trade would be a more appropriate banner. Then there was a battle about whether the aid bit should be 'double aid' or 'more and better aid'. The push to call for better as well as more aid was indicative of a growing desire among campaigners to talk more openly about the difficulties of making aid work, and the growing unease of many experts about how effective aid is as a way of helping reduce poverty. Eventually, those calling for 'more and better aid' won the battle. But they did not win the war.

Two camps quickly emerged. On the one hand were those who, working closely with the UK government, focused on delivering 'results' in 2005. Others were more interested in getting the analysis right, and were prepared to accept less in immediate 'deliverables'. The UK government was present behind the scenes throughout the campaign. When the Make Poverty History manifesto had already been signed off and was going to press, a call from one of Gordon Brown's senior advisers led to last-minute changes. The adviser asked for the manifesto to contain an explicit reference to the need for $50 billion extra in aid, rather than simply calling for aid to be doubled. This reasonably harmless request was granted, but it was an early sign that somehow British aid charities had found themselves in the unusual position of launching a huge campaign calling for policies the government was already planning to announce. Interestingly, the relationship between governments responding to pressure to increase aid and actually helping to augment that pressure is quite complex. In the United Kingdom at least, the government set out an explicit agenda not only to raise aid levels but to build public support for such rises. It did this by working closely with NGOs and by producing and collaborating in analyses purporting to show the effectiveness of aid in reducing poverty, most noticeably in 2005 with the report of Tony Blair's Africa Commission. It may therefore be more appropriate to say that rather than responding to public calls for rises in aid the British government responded to public calls to do something about poverty and sought to persuade people that aid was the best way of doing it. The need to engage actively in building public support for increases in aid is testament to the high levels of scepticism about the effectiveness of aid, particularly fears that it is used corruptly.

At first glance the Make Poverty History campaign was about more than just more aid. As well as the aid demand the campaign had two other prongs – calls for debt cancellation and trade justice. It appeared that the message had developed from the days of just forking out a fiver for Africa. But despite this apparent three-pronged message (or four-pronged if you include better aid) the reality was somewhat different. Looking back on the campaign, the concessions wrung from the G8 and other rich countries were promises to give more money. What about giving better? Better aid was a key campaign demand and is talked about endlessly in development circles. But if you ask people who wore the white Make Poverty History wristband how the campaign thought aid could be made better, it becomes clear how relatively little commotion was made about the issue. The manifesto called for more money to be spent on basic services, the untying of aid to purchases from donor countries, the democratizing of the World Bank and IMF, an end to undemocratic and harmful aid conditions, and measures to make aid delivery more predictable. Did Make Poverty History, and the global campaigns that worked with it, lead to progress on these points? In short, no. Most people knew only that more money was to be sent to Africa. When the Live 8 concerts came along, any stubborn attempts to maintain a more sophisticated message were finally blown out of the water.

On trade, nothing significant was achieved. The Make Poverty History manifesto called for an end to Western export subsidies, laws to better regulate the actions of multinational businesses profiting at the expense of people and the environment, and an end to the imposition of neoliberal trade policies on poor countries. It is not surprising that these goals were not achieved – they were ambitious – but it is doubtful that the Make Poverty History campaign even added much pressure on rich governments to change. The idea was to focus on trade issues in the second half of the year, but by then most of the momentum had been lost – the film stars were busy doing other things, the campaigning money had dried up, and the key moment, the G8 Gleneagles meeting, had been and gone. Aid had stolen the show.

There were some important achievements on debt cancellation, although much more is still needed. About twenty (mostly African) countries had all the debt they owed to the IMF, World Bank and African Development Bank wiped out. Debt relief is better than aid. It not only frees up money to spend on development that would otherwise be sent abroad, it frees countries from reliance on donors, affording them more autonomy over policy decisions. Aid does the opposite. Unfortunately, in order to qualify for debt relief, countries have to jump through policy hoops set up by the creditors. This has historically undermined the good that debt relief should do. The 2005 debt deals did free a number African governments from some of their reliance on donors. Aid accounted for 29 per cent of the Zambian government budget in 2006 which, though still very high, is the lowest ratio for some years.[35] The debt cancellation deals reduced aid dependency slightly, but there is a still a very long way to go. Countries that have benefited from debt relief, or are experiencing growing revenues on the back of high oil and commodity prices, should capitalize on this new-found freedom by seeking alternative funding sources, particularly domestically. Increasing the aid to government revenue ratio again, by doubling aid to Africa, would be a step backwards. But that is precisely what aid campaigners are calling for. Bob Geldof declared the summit a success, giving the aid deal 10 out of 10 and the debt deal 8 out of 10, despite clear instructions from the Make Poverty History campaign team that on all fronts (aid, debt and trade) the promises from the G8 did not meet even the minimum demands of the campaign. This turned simmering discontent with the way some of the Make Poverty History campaign's leaders, especially the celebrity circuit, were undermining well-thought-through campaign demands, into public dissent. But in a sense Bob Geldof was right. According to certain criteria, little more could have been hoped for from the G8 summit. For Geldof success was measured in dollar signs, and appeared to involve little analysis of the complex range of impacts that aid can have on poor people in Africa.

Why does the international development community continue to emphasize more over better aid? In part because there is honest disagreement about the best way for Africa to reduce poverty. The view that aid is a vital part of the answer is held by some very serious people. But there are other reasons, including poor analysis and, unfortunately, an element of self-interest. In Britain, as in many countries, international charities are one of the most respected sectors. Rightly so. Their work is of a very high quality and makes a real difference to millions of people around the world. When they speak they are seen as independent and trustworthy, with no vested interests. On almost all issues this is indeed the case. But aid is one of the few issues, if not the only issue, on which international charities are beholden to other interests, and on which they do not speak with the same candour as they do on other subjects. To take an analogy, foreign direct investment (FDI) is a complicated issue in development. It is wrong to imply, as some governments do, that it is always a good thing. Sometimes it is a positive influence on poverty reduction, sometimes irrelevant, and sometimes downright harmful. Respected charities therefore take a balanced position, promoting FDI where appropriate, and criticizing it where it is not. The impacts of trade liberalization are complex as well. Sometimes it can help, but often it does not – it depends on a variety of factors within a country and outside it.

On the whole range of development issues sensible charities carry out research and take a balanced line based on the interests of the poor and marginalized.

On aid it is different. Charities do not find it so easy to criticize aid when it is necessary to do so. There are vested interests at play. Increases in government aid usually mean increases in charity coffers. Cuts in donor government aid overall would probably mean cuts in charity budgets, as most charities receive large parts of their funding from government. Around 35 per cent of Save the Children UK's charitable expenditure came from public authorities, mostly governments, in 2007.[36] But even this is small compared with some of the big US charities. Care USA relies on the US and other governments for well over half of its $600 million annual operating expenses.[37] Many charities are equally concerned about the effect criticizing aid might have on private donations. Even though the main criticisms are of government-to-government aid, they are worried that the public will not really notice the difference and that donations will drop as a result. These are valid concerns – it is vital for charities to stay strong in order to do their important work on the ground and to keep the pressure on those in power to do better for the world's poor. But the balance has to be struck: the mandate of charities is to speak the unpalatable truth, without fear or favour. It is not only financial ties with governments that muffle NGOs. Gordon Brown's closest adviser on international development, now a government minister, served on Oxfam's board for many years before finally relinquishing her duties after the Make Poverty History campaign. Many NGO workers spend part of their career in the government sector.

Many charities and experts in the field have strong criticisms of aid practices and their overall effects on poverty and human rights. It is common to hear private criticism. There has been much concern, for example, about the wrong-headed nature of some of the conditions USAID attaches to the money it donates for AIDS work, which are based on ideological positions on abstinence and prostitution. But only a handful have been brave enough to speak out in public, most fearing the repercussions on their bottom line. A fair amount of reports criticizing aid do emerge, but the nervousness about undermining public support for aid is palpable, and they seldom get well publicized. A groundbreaking new series of reports has been established by ActionAid called *Real Aid*, which breaks down what aid really looks like and reveals how much is wasted or misused.[38] It has played an important role in moving the aid quality agenda on in the United Kingdom and abroad. But the decision to continue to call for aid increases is made before the analysis is done, so whatever the evidence, the central message is the same: give more. Meanwhile conditionalities have been the target of coordinated campaigns for decades and continue to be so. But while many African NGOs seriously question whether aid and debt relief benefit Africa given the harmful conditions attached, Western charities do not tend to allow that question to be asked – it is too subversive. Charities have a way of criticizing aid for pages and pages and then turning round and calling for more. One can add to these internal pressures the simple fact that it is hard to change course and admit that you are wrong. Charities have been campaigning to increase aid for as long as most have existed – it is in their blood. The target of 0.7 per cent of GNI is set in stone. To admit to the public now that, actually, aid in many countries in Africa is not doing much good and might be doing a good deal of damage is never going to be easy. But in reality the analysis hardly ever gets to that stage. The possible truth waiting to be uncovered is so unpalatable that debate is ended before it begins.

Another reason aid usually comes out as the campaign of choice is that many NGOs want to engage in campaigning but feel uncomfortable taking on complex economic and political issues, or overly challenging the status quo. Giving more money could hardly be described as that. Aid is deliverable, measurable and easily explainable. Everyone knows what it means to give or lend money; more aid can be (and is being) delivered by governments. These are important qualities for campaigners and potential funders across the world. We all want to change the world, but some things are more possible than others. In an increasingly target-oriented culture results mean more funding, and that includes campaign results. In the debt negotiations of the late 1990s, often hailed as a great success for poor countries, there was a split in the Jubilee debt movement when Northern organizations backed the plan offered by the donor (or, in this case, creditor) countries, emphasizing the important fiscal benefits of the possible debt cancellation. Many Southern NGOs, while recognizing the need for debt relief, were much more sceptical about what was on offer – the conditions in the Highly Indebted Poor Country (HIPC) initiative were as stringent and harmful as they always had been. Were they a price worth paying? Looking back at a decade of varying quantities of debt relief but effectively implemented conditions, perhaps Northern NGOs were too quick to go for the deliverable result. Perhaps the Southern NGOs were right.

Aid giving is by no means entirely about political strategy and vested interests. It is possible to argue very sensibly that for all the harm it does do, aid overall benefits its recipients – this is certainly the majority position in the aid community. While many acknowledge the critiques of aid laid out in this book, they would not agree with its conclusions that aid should be reduced in much of Africa. The worry, though, is that this judgement is not being made in balanced isolation, as are most charity policies, but with heavy pressures on one side of the scales. Charities, on the whole, do incredible work and deserve nothing but admiration and respect. But on this issue they have got it wrong. The likelihood of big charities changing their mind on doubling aid in the short term is nil. But they might take their feet off the pedal, and start the slow process of rowing back from a fervently held position; they might acknowledge that other issues are more deserving of attention. Because until the clamour for more aid dies down, the hard decisions that really matter will barely get a look in.

9 | What is to be done?

Most African countries are dependent on aid. They need foreign financial assistance simply to keep afloat. No country in the world can survive entirely independent of other countries, nor should it want to. Even the mighty United States depends on other countries for its well-being, whether that is through political support, trade or other ties (most notably global purchases of US government bonds – including by developing countries – which fund the budget and balance of payments deficits). But the kind of severe dependence described in this book is not mutually beneficial. It is unlikely that aid increases to Africa will have a significant impact on poverty reduction and long-term development. On the contrary, aid has frequently damaged development prospects in Africa and further increases in aid could make the situation even worse. Instead, African leaders should again plot a course towards independence. Rather than setting the goal of doubling aid by 2015, donors and recipients should together agree to do the opposite. Perhaps they could aim to halve it by 2020, while taking the other measures necessary – outlined in this chapter – to fill the financing gap and support poverty reduction.

Everyone agrees aid should eventually be reduced: the question is, when. You are unlikely to find a straight answer. The nearest position among Western politicians and campaigners to a commitment to bring aid down comes from the proponents of the International Finance Facility (the IFF) – most vocally, the UK government – who have allowed the implication to surface that if the IFF helps donors double aid by 2015, then post-2015 aid could begin to fall.[1] But even with this scenario, the most ambitious one around, we can expect aid to fall only gradually over time, perhaps reaching today's levels again by, say, 2030. That means another twenty years or so of today's levels of dependency before Africa even *begins* to recover its autonomy. Perhaps the time to begin reducing aid has already come. Africa needs less and better aid.

But cold turkey is not an option (nor is it at all likely). If Africa is desperately short of cash at the moment, reducing aid too quickly would make the shortfall even more drastic. It would spell financial turmoil for African governments and disaster for millions of poor people who rely on aid money to survive. What is required is not a sudden break, but a deliberate change of direction, moving away from aid dependence. This will not be easy and will require brave leadership focused on longer time horizons than the next general election. But it is possible if donor countries take the appropriate supporting actions. Aid advocates frequently adopt the following non sequitur: there is a financing gap, therefore we need more aid. This is not the case. Therefore we need more money. Those mega-calculations (x billion dollars = y million lives saved) are not entirely misguided. One of the latest estimates is that for an extra $27.1 billion invested in the health sector in 2010, almost 5 million lives could be saved globally.[2] That kind of money could have that kind of impact. But it should not be aid money. The unadvertised costs of aid, as we have seen, too frequently outweigh the benefits. So the question is where should the money come from?

Development finance: a simple equation

Net resources for development = domestic resources + inflows − outflows

Development finance means finding the money needed to pay for development. Resources already in a country can be supplemented with money and resources from abroad (aid, loans, foreign investment and, increasingly, remittances). But it is important to remember that billions of dollars flow out of Africa every year as well, destined for rich countries. The most famous outflows are debt repayments, but there are many others. So the amount of money available to a country to spend every year on development depends on how much domestic money is available, and how much money has entered or exited the economy. The focus of development policy is too often on maximizing inflows. People in the development business sometimes even loosely use the phrase 'development finance' to mean money transferred from the North to the South. This focus on inflows permeates the thinking of governments on both left and right, as well as development professionals and civil society campaigners. Every major campaign in the West has focused on inflows, with the exception of the debt campaign. Inflows are important, but they are only one of the three factors in the development finance equation, and they can sometimes be the least important of the three. We should be spending more time on the other two: minimizing outflows and maximizing domestic resources.

Plugging the leaks

Before we put money in our pockets, we check that there are no holes in them. In the same way, before we look at how Africa can make more money we need to look at one of the great under-investigated issues of African development – how it can keep hold of the money it already has. Africa at the moment is like a leaky bucket – billions of dollars are lost to Africa every year in illicit capital flight, investment abroad, debt repayments and bolstering central bank reserves, far more than arrive in the form of aid and foreign investment. Because much of this money is moved around illegally, using questionable accounting practices and the global network of tax havens, it is hard to know exactly how much money is involved, so we should not be surprised if some of the numbers don't tally – they are broad estimates from a range of sources. It is astonishing but true that the World Bank and IMF, which have data for almost everything, do not have figures, not even official estimates, for what is Africa's gravest financial problem. While the attention of the world's governments and campaigners remains on aid, this scandalous haemorrhaging of African cash stays off the radar screens.

Recent estimates suggest that capital flight from Africa totalled more than $400 billion (in 2004 dollars) between 1970 and 2004.[3]

When you add imputed interest earnings, that figure passes $600 billion in funds lost to the continent. Africa has received $500 billion in aid since 1960.[4] While volatile, capital flight appears to be a growing problem, with losses doubling from $15 billion in 1991 to just under $30 billion in 2003 (although they fell significantly the following year).[5] These figures are higher than aid receipts, especially given that much aid money is not actually a cash transfer to Africa but is spent in donor country economies.[6] Experts believe there is a direct link with loans, arguing that for every $1 of loans Africa has received since 1970, between 60–80 cents has left the continent that same year in capital flight, transforming public borrowing, paid back by the state, into the private wealth of a few.[7]

Some of the African money invested abroad is done so quite legitimately. In a globalized world investors from any country can weigh up risk and potential return across the world and decide where to place their savings. If they see investments in Africa as too risky, or unlikely to deliver as much profit, it is natural that they will invest elsewhere. But the bulk of money spirited away from the continent is done so either illegally or in a manner that most people would consider underhand, even if it is not explicitly illegal. According to some estimates, fake and mispriced trade transactions (whereby exports are underpriced and imports are overpriced) account for illegal capital flight of between $150–200 billion every year globally.[8] And the practice appears to be on the increase. A study of questionable trade transactions between Africa and the United Status alone, from small-scale business partners to large multinational companies, found that net capital outflows grew from around $2 billion in 1996 to just under $5 billion in 2005.[9] According to Raymond Baker, author of the most authoritative analysis on this issue, around 60 per cent of African trade transactions are intentionally mispriced by an average of more than 11 per cent each year.[10] Apart from the diversion of vast resources from possible domestic investment towards investment in countries that are already rich, there is a second problem with illicit capital flight

– it goes untaxed, thus wresting billions of dollars away from potential development funds.

Another important part of this outflow is money gained from corruption. According to African Union estimates, $148 billion leaves the continent every year because of corruption, equivalent to over a fifth of the continent's GDP.[11] Corruption need not necessarily be damaging to a country's economic development. Many countries in today's world are highly corrupt and yet are doing very well economically, just as corruption in Britain was rife in the nineteenth century during a period of rapid development.[12] The problem is not corruption per se but what happens to the money. Is it invested at home, as it was in nineteenth-century Britain, or abroad? Money stolen by public officials in Africa tends to flow abroad, and only 10–20 per cent of capital outflows ever return to the continent.[13] The existence of easy mechanisms to hide money encourages corruption that might otherwise not have taken place.

As always the role of African governments is paramount in dealing with this crisis. They need to persuade Africans to invest their money (whether corruptly gained or not) in Africa. Leading economist Dani Rodrik has argued that 'often the key [to economic growth] is a set of targeted policy interventions that kindle the animal spirits of domestic investors'.[14] Greater political stability and effective property rights will help to stem capital flight, but the neoliberal dream of low-to-no tax and low-to-no regulation is unlikely to benefit Africans in the long run.

Without a clear change in rich country policies, it is difficult to envisage how African governments will be able to stem the flows. The part played by foreign governments is crucial. First, they need to hand back the stolen money that is sitting in Western bank accounts benefiting Western economies. On some estimates African political elites hold about $700–800 billion outside Africa.[15] Occasionally there is a major legal case and large amounts of money are returned to Africa. Swiss banks have finally paid back most of the money stolen by Sani Abacha, Nigeria's dictator in the 1990s.[16] Nigeria's Economic and Financial Crimes

Commission has recovered $5 billion and convicted eighty-two people since 2003.[17] But these are the exceptions not the rule. There is an estimated $1 billion looted by Sani Abacha still in the United Kingdom.[18] Even more important than returning the money now is stemming the leakage in the years to come. Rich countries need to shut down tax havens – they serve no useful purpose and their only real use is to help businesses and individuals hide money and avoid paying tax. Governments around the world lose over $250 billion a year in lost tax revenues because of this dubious system – so rich governments are losing too.[19] Not to mention victims of terrorism and organized crime – the tax haven network is used by all the world's biggest criminal and terrorist networks, as one would expect. But the biggest losers, as usual, are the poor, as they see money that could have been invested in development spirited abroad. International accounting standards need to be tightened to reduce the amount of fake and mispriced transactions – by far the biggest tool for moving money out of Africa. Why do rich countries refuse to act? Simple. They are under pressure from big businesses and banks who are making billions from the system to leave it alone. And there is little pressure from anywhere else to do the opposite. Campaigners are busy calling for more aid.

Rich countries need to deal with corruption too. The demand side is well known – the African recipients in corrupt deals. But what about supply? Who is offering the bribes, and who is laundering the money? When it comes to corruption, the rules of the market do not always apply. Supply does not necessarily *meet* demand, it creates it. In other words, civil institutions that may have been relatively uncorrupted may become corrupt when large amounts of money start to swill around, either because of foreign investment (especially in oil, mining and construction) or because of aid receipts and loans. The hypocrisy is rampant. While self-righteously chastising Africans, rich countries are encouraging the theft of Africa's wealth, through inaction or active involvement. There have been moves, led by the UK government, voluntarily to open up secret dealings between foreign business and African governments; this is laudable, but transparency must be made mandatory.[20] And while some companies say they want to reveal the deals with their host governments, those very governments are reluctant for this to happen. In Equatorial Guinea, for example, the spending of oil earnings is an official state secret.[21] In such circumstances ethical companies should think about removing their investments until the books are opened. Laws need to be changed in many countries so that such actions do not contradict a company's legal duty to maximize value. Moves to clamp down on corruption from the supply side could have huge and beneficial effects on Africa's economy and society, and in many cases it will simply mean enforcing the present rules better. Decisive action is required, but will be taken only if politicians feel the pressure to act.

Next on the list of leaks is the build-up by many African central banks of large foreign exchange reserves. Most countries in the world have been stocking up reserves in a context of increased capital market volatility and the threat of investors rapidly shifting their money. While the increase in Africa as a whole has been limited compared with the huge reserve bolstering occurring in Asia and Latin America, Africa saw its international reserves double from about $30 billion in 1999 to over $60 billion in 2004. As most of these reserves are in US treasury bills, Africa is getting a very low return on its investment – T-bills are risk free but very low yielding. Invested elsewhere, these billions of dollars could be building infrastructure and training nurses and teachers, instead of propping up the US's huge budget deficit. Joseph Stiglitz has suggested setting up a pool of hard currency that countries could call on in a crisis, repaying it afterwards, and thus avoiding the need to keep such big reserves.[22] Another proposal is the use of a rapidly escalating tax on capital outflows, which governments could impose in cases of investor panic.[23]

The final leak is debt repayment. Countries borrow money to help finance their expenditures but in the long term this often doesn't work out very well. Between 1970 and 2002 Africa received $540 billion in loans. Despite paying back nearly $550 billion to its creditors during that time, interest charges meant it still had a debt of $295 billion at the end of 2002.[24] In 2005, low-income countries paid out about $120 million a day in debt repayments.[25] Despite some important (given fairly low expectations) debt cancellation deals since the late 1990s, debt repayments remain high in Africa. What makes it worse is that many of the loans were illegitimate, sometimes actually illegal, and were often wasted or stolen. Propping up ugly dictators has been a habit of Western money for a long time. From the apartheid regime in South Africa to Mobutu in Zaire, money has been lent to some very unsavoury regimes and used for repression, not development. Unethical creditors who lent the money are now entrenching the harm they did in the past by demanding repayment of those very debts, or the debts incurred to pay the previous debts. The examples are too numerous to list.[26] The protection of debt servicing as a priority government expenditure while basic needs are not being met is immoral. Rich countries should cancel Africa's debt once and for all.

Untapped opportunities

The main problems with aid are its impacts on policies and institutions. Stemming the vast outflow of money and resources from Africa would bring none of these adverse effects – it would simply bolster state coffers and promote domestic investment. The macroeconomic effects would in some cases be similar to aid and would therefore require careful management. They could be offset by aid reductions.

The other side of the coin is maximizing the amount of money Africa makes, and using it more productively. Fundamentally, African governments need to raise domestic revenues. If they grow faster than in the past, after adopting more economically viable policies, and if they reintroduce trade taxes where appropriate and impose ambitious but achievable taxes on big companies, especially foreign multinationals, their overall tax take will rise. But serious efforts to increase individual taxation are needed as well, not only to increase government revenue but also to improve the crucial state–citizen relationship. In an ideal world, everyone would pay something, so that everyone has the right to demand accountable government. Ultimately a strong personal income tax collection system is needed. But that is a long way from being possible in much of Africa where people do not receive an income, or do so in an informal way that is hard to register. African governments will have to decide the best long-term strategy for raising taxes. But their efforts must be supported by rich countries who presently encourage developing countries to compete for foreign investment by lowering taxes, and foster an international tax system that can be easily abused. According to South Africa's finance minister, Trevor Manuel, 'It is a contradiction to support increased development assistance, yet turn a blind eye to actions by multinationals and others that undermine the tax base of a developing country.'[27]

Raising revenue is only a part of the equation. Better use of savings is also key. UNCTAD, which has been an important voice over the years challenging the hubristic and now discredited neoliberalism of other international institutions, focused its 2007 annual report on Africa on domestic resource mobilization. Its findings will surprise many. Far from being short of cash, African banks are actually too liquid. But they are not using the money they have productively. African businesses cite lack of credit as their most important constraint, along with lack of infrastructure, institutions and skills.[28] The lack of good information systems on potential borrowers and systems to enforce repayment inhibit moneylending, which is the way savings are turned into productive investments. Additionally, most banks in Africa are now in foreign hands, following financial liberalization as part of the structural adjustment reforms package. In Botswana, Guinea-Bissau and Lesotho all banking assets, worryingly, are owned by foreign banks.[29] According to UNCTAD, 'These banks lend to larger borrowers such as the public sector, large enterprises and wealthy households. They do not have mechanisms well suited to catering to the needs of small, low-income and mostly agricultural and rural-based economic agents, despite the fact that these agents constitute the backbone of African economies.'[30] Reforms in the African banking sector have improved management in some cases, but banking services for rural households and the informal sector (by far the largest part of Africa's private sector) have suffered. Most of Africa's wealth never reaches the formal banking sector. Developing more informal and semi-formal saving and investment mechanisms needs to be a top priority for Africa, with the goal of eventually making better links with the formal sector. Changes in these areas are feasible if governments prioritize them.

What about foreign sources of money? Some analysts emphasize the increasing (though still small) foreign investment flows to Africa and appear to equate them with progress and poverty reduction. FDI can be an important part of development finance, if well regulated, but it tends to be concentrated in areas of the economy, such as extractive industries, which create few jobs and may have only limited knock-on effects to other parts of the economy. On top of this, countries that rely on foreign investment must face the real possibility that even if new investment exceeds repatriated profits at the moment, the tables may soon turn. In Nigeria, Angola and South Africa profit remittances outweigh actual inflows, while in the rest of Africa the net transfers on foreign investment are minimal. The question with foreign investment, as with all development finance, is, 'Who is benefiting?' Foreign direct investment in Africa, like aid, is also quite volatile, making it a dangerous prop in a development strategy. Not so remittances, which are growing steadily and do not depend on the economic context in the recipient country. Africa receives the lowest level of remittances of any region (only 5 per cent of the global total) although the official figure of $4 billion a year is certainly a substantial underestimate.[31] Although only directly benefiting the lucky recipients, there is evidence that remittances make an important contribution to development. Up to 80 per cent are used for consumption and schooling in Africa, but they are increasingly being used to finance small and medium-sized enterprises and small infrastructure projects.[32]

Policies are needed to promote the use of remittances into productive investment.

From dependency to independence

The pull of neoliberalism has been broken. Its failings scar Africa and shame the West. Development is more complicated than neoliberals (and neo-cons) would have us believe. It is time for a new era of intellectual openness. In contrast to thirty years of clamping down on choice, let the decades ahead be the decades of choice, of experimentation again, and of sovereignty.

For some more advanced countries in Africa, economic liberalization will be the right path to follow, while for others it will be important to protect and subsidize industries that could be important sources of jobs and wealth, now and in the future. The neoliberal sneering at policies to protect infant industries, common only a few years ago, is falling silent as Africa fails to industrialize. History demonstrates that government support is necessary if countries are to diversify their production away from basic natural resources towards more complex products. Usually there is a point at which economies benefit from more competition, as the East Asian tigers have shown. How fast should economies be liberalized? *It depends.*

While exports play a vital part in any economy, the pressure to increase exports has to be balanced against the need to ensure food security. Kenya was self-sufficient in food in the 1980s but is now a net food importer. As food prices rise across the world, consumers will be hit, but it could also mean new opportunities for farmers. How should African governments respond to this challenge? Perhaps some have strong enough economies to take the risk of not growing all their own food. Others may need to balance the trend towards exports with an emphasis on food production, which can also, of course, be processed and exported, providing an important step towards industrialization. *It depends.*

Sometimes strict rules and hefty taxes should be applied to multinational companies and foreign investors in order to maximize their poverty-reducing impact in a country, and minimize the environmental and social harm they sometimes cause. At other times, offering ten-year tax holidays might even be a good idea. *It depends.* Sometimes privatization works, with benefits both to shareholders and consumers. Sometimes it costs jobs, stokes corruption and is less efficient. *It depends.* Usually imposing upfront payments for basic services dissuades the poorest from using them. Sometimes asking service users to pay enhances the service and increases take-up. *It depends.* Sometimes opening up government procurement to full competition will benefit state and citizen. Sometimes it will harm key industries. Sometimes it will do both. *It depends.*

What is important on these and the whole range of other difficult decisions governments have to make is that the choices are made in Africa by accountable and effective governments. African governments need to develop alternative economic plans to the blueprints they have been following. They need to build analytical capacity. They need to nurture better democratic systems, responding to domestic constituencies rather than foreign powers. Most important are the capacity and freedom to try things, known in the jargon as 'policy space'. African governments should regulate and formulate policy as they see fit, not as they are told to do by donors that stand to benefit from certain economic policies. They should reap the rewards when things go well, and accept responsibility when they do not. They should learn from their successes and mistakes.

But the barriers are tremendous. It is hard to overstate the constraints holding African governments back from taking on donors who have the power to cause hardship for whole countries, not to mention political careers, and who have frequently shown their willingness to use it. Power is the theme that underpins many of the arguments in this book. The most important contributions from those who want to overhaul the aid system (most people in the aid system want to overhaul the aid system!) are those that recognize the fundamental power relationships at play, and that therefore emphasize the need to find ways to rebalance them. In my view, African governments need to reduce their dependence on aid to have the power to set their own development agenda. But they cannot do it alone. Donors need to stop using the aid system as an instrument of control, and instead to support new ways of mobilizing money for poverty in Africa. There will always be a limit to African autonomy until action is taken at an international level to free up other forms of development finance. If donors are driven by humanitarian concern, they must recognize that at present their efforts are not producing the required results. If they are motivated by narrow self-interest, it is up to voters to demand more enlightened policies and to press for change.

Rich governments use a number of tools apart from aid to bribe African countries to do certain things. True, if aid is taken out of the equation there is less leverage and African countries will have more sovereignty over their decisions. This is what happens when large amounts of debt are cancelled – as well as getting a fiscal breathing space, governments depend less on foreign financing and can take more autonomous decisions. But there are plenty of ways left for rich countries to pile on the pressure. At the most extreme, Western countries have a record of supporting coups against governments, democratic or otherwise, when they disapprove of what they are doing. Usually the pressure is more subtle. The most important way rich countries have enforced certain policies in Africa, apart from the aid system, has been trade negotiations both within the WTO and outside it. The European Union is currently using the promise of better trade access through Economic Partnership Agreements (EPAs) to pressurize African governments to adopt policies most do not want to adopt. Just like aid conditionalities, this pressure undermines democratic accountability and the ability of African countries to make decisions in their own interests. In fact even EU aid priorities, according to the EU's Trade Commissioner, will be directed towards helping implement EPAs.[33] Rich countries genuinely concerned with development and poverty reduction in Africa would make concessions without demanding concessions in return.

Donor governments will take a good deal of persuading to change their bad habits. Sometimes long-term strategic interests, allied to humanitarian concern, trump short-term interests, which are frequently governed by what big business wants. But sometimes they do not. In what is a notoriously difficult context, African governments must bravely carve out a firm direction. When countries arrive at the negotiating table with clear ideological preferences and viable policy suggestions, and when they demonstrate democratic legitimacy, it becomes harder for donors to take control of the process. There are some examples of African governments standing up to donors in this way, especially when they form a negotiating bloc. It becomes even harder for donors to impose their will when recipients are prepared to refuse aid if they are not content with the overall package. The short-term difficulties such decisions will cause will be serious. It is hard to know when the right time to start reducing aid dependence will be, but there is no reason to believe things will be easier in the future, especially if Africa becomes even more dependent on aid. The best time might be now.

Should rich countries just keep the aid money?

This book has argued that less money year on year should be transferred from donor accounts to Africa. But what should be done with all the money saved? Those who argue that rich countries are miserly in the amount of money they spend on the very poor are right. The disparities are shocking and shameful. Should we really give less?

First we need to get away from the idea that rich country generosity should be measured in aid dollars. As we have seen, aid is not only cheap and easy; it is also a very good investment for the donors. Making unilateral concessions in trade deals with African countries, accepting more taxes and tighter regulations of multinational businesses, relaxing intellectual property right laws so that copies can be made, closing down tax havens and returning stolen money – the costs of these policies to people in donor countries will be greater than those of aid in the short term.

That would be real generosity and it would make a real difference, rather than passing on small amounts of our vast wealth every year in a way that often does more harm than good. In the long term everyone would benefit from a prosperous Africa. In 2005 at the post-G8 press conference at Gleneagles, the UK's Prime Minister, Tony Blair, got away with describing the relationship of the G8 with the developing world as one based on 'charity'.[34] It isn't. Charity may play a part but good old-fashioned exploitation remains a dominant feature as well. Donor economies continue to do well at the expense of African economies because of the policy regimes they have successfully imposed which facilitate better profits for foreign investors and better terms of trade. It will take much more than aid increases to demonstrate that a genuine shift in perspective has taken place.

Nevertheless, there is a pot of money called 'aid to Africa' and it should be reduced. At the same time we should ramp up our spending on development in Africa, far surpassing the 0.7 per cent target. The two are not incompatible. We *should* give more, but not as traditional 'aid to Africa'. The problems identified in this book occur when money is transferred from one jurisdiction to another. Rather than transferring so much money to poor countries, we should be spending money on the development of new technologies, including life-saving drugs, renewable and clean energy, and other global public goods. One thing that is clear from economic history, especially looking at the twentieth century during which many countries saw rapid growth and a new stage of globalization began, is that technology travels fast. The mobile phone, for example, is revolutionizing Africa, making discussions about installing the expensive infrastructure of land lines redundant. An investment in technologies that matter to Africans is an investment in Africa.

Nowhere is this more evident than in the field of health. Improvements in medicines and healthcare techniques have been responsible for vast improvements in living standards across the world, not just in rich countries, over the last hundred years. Although the biggest improvements in health (such as primary healthcare, mass vaccination campaigns, oral rehydration therapy) have relied on much more than new technology, scientific advances have been vital in many areas, and have in turn depended on a combination of public and private investment. Notwithstanding the remarkable progress that has been made there are some disgraceful anomalies, the most famous being the difference in access to life-saving HIV drugs in the rich world compared with Africa. A large part of the problem is the unjust patent regime that has made it harder for today's poor countries to do what today's rich countries did when they were poor – copy foreign technologies.[35] Global patent laws must be urgently reversed. But another part of the solution is putting more public money into medical research. This would mean relatively more money spent on things that matter to most human beings (such as malaria and diarrhoea) and less on things that matter to a small percentage (like nose-jobs). The world's major drugs companies devote 90 per cent of their research time and money to rich world diseases that affect less than 10 per cent of the world's population.[36] More publicly funded research would also mean fewer problems with patents.[37] To improve health for the poorest will take much more than cheaper drugs. Countries need to develop good health systems for the long term – probably a much higher priority. But developing good health systems needs to be handled by the country concerned – aid money can do as much harm as good. Donors should be encouraged to focus on the good they *can* do with their cash.

Another area in which more money needs urgently to be invested in research and development is climate change, a problem donor countries largely created but which the poor in Africa are now paying for.[38] The fight against poverty and injustice is long. Anyone who has worked in this field for any length of time knows that for every step forward new challenges appear, new problems to overcome. 'Make poverty history' was always a great slogan, but never a very tangible objective. The fight against catastrophic climate change is different. It is time-bound. Alongside all the political changes needed to save our planet, and especially those inhabitants least able to protect themselves, vastly more money should be spent on clean solutions. One of the most important things that rich countries can do to help Africa is to reduce global carbon emissions by slashing their own and helping poor countries develop more cleanly. Alternative energy solutions that do not harm our planet are perfectly within the ken of today's scientists, but more money needs to be ploughed into developing them, adapting them to developing country conditions, and making them available at a cheap enough price to roll them out. Not just millions but billions of dollars – a substantial part of today's aid package. Appropriate micro-renewable energy technologies have the potential to transform rural development in Africa. Again, developing the science is only a part of it. Solar panels in the middle of a Chadian village need to be maintained, and that means setting up support networks and training people. But the technology is a vital first step.

Real generosity

Those who question whether aid is really doing much good, and may even be doing harm, are sometimes met with the withering response – well, we have to do something. This is reminiscent of the classic syllogism from the British sitcom *Yes, Minister*: 'Something must be done; this is something; therefore we must do it!' The implication is that the options are aid or nothing. But this is nonsense. There are many important strategies that African countries should be adopting to reduce their dependence on aid and forge a new path, and that rich countries should be adopting to play their part in Africa's development. In fact, the overwhelming focus on aid has meant that for too long these far more important issues have been left in the shadows. In this final chapter we have touched on a few of them – but there are many more.

Today's global intellectual property rights regime, which protects the rich and harms the poor, is not, as is sometimes implied, a normal and inevitable part of a modern capitalist and globalized economy. It has been constructed by developed countries to lock in their advantages and is in urgent need of reform. Africa is not ready for the unjust patent laws being imposed on it. The injustices are most glaring in the field of health. The beneficiaries of global intellectual property rights agreements are multinational drugs companies. The losers are those too poor to purchase life-saving drugs Westerners now take for granted.

While the rich world dismantles subsidies and trade barriers in Africa, it still spends almost $350 billion a year subsidizing its agriculture, thus depressing global prices and unfairly putting African farmers out of business.[39] Coupled with this, importing countries often disincentivize industrial development in Africa by protecting their markets with higher tariffs on textiles, clothing and food, precisely the labour-intensive products that offer developing countries the first step up the technology ladder. Undoing these unfair arrangements is achievable in the short term and it would have important consequences for many farmers and exporters in Africa, although it is important to note that as prices rise with a reduction in subsidies, consumers in Africa would be hit as well, making the equation very complicated, with both winners and losers.

Complementing better domestic regulation by African governments, rich world governments should regulate multinational businesses based in their countries so as to ensure that negative and environmental impacts are reduced. Rich countries regularly ignore African countries' sovereign decisions, as we have seen. But when it comes to acting to stop multinationals violating basic social and environmental standards they hide behind the excuse of 'sovereignty'. Pollution is acceptable in poor countries, the argument goes, if the poor country government allows it or is not strong enough to prevent it. Different standards will apply, most obviously in wage levels, and minimum standards must not be used as a kind of de facto protectionism. But companies should be made to abide by international norms using legal mechanisms.

More and more skilled people are leaving Africa to start a new life in richer countries which lack trained professionals in some sectors. Efforts must be made to curb this 'brain drain'. When there is a small stock of educated and trained people, as is the case in much of Africa, the cost of losing them is high. No amount of remittances can make up for an absolute shortage of doctors and nurses. In some African countries as many as 40 per cent of university graduates emigrate to rich countries and only a few return.[40] Up to three-quarters of Zambia's qualified doctors leave the country, while Malawi now has just 266 doctors for 13 million people.[41] The tens of thousands of dollars spent training each doctor are effectively subsidizing rich countries health systems, while back home the lack of trained staff means AIDS and other diseases continue to go unchecked.

Conflict remains an ongoing tragedy in Africa, scarring the lives and life-chances of millions of people. It is also one of the main barriers to development and poverty reduction. Oxfam claims that 38 per cent of the world's armed conflicts are being fought in Africa, and estimates that armed conflict costs Africa around $18 billion per year, roughly half what it receives in aid.[42] More needs to be done to curb the arms trade, both legal and illegal, which has made Africa the world's leading recipient of small arms. This is possible, though it will have political and economic costs. The five permanent members of the UN Security Council (China, the United States, Russia, France and the United Kingdom) are also the world's five leading arms exporters.

There is not space in this book to dwell on all the various ways in which rich countries could do more for Africa. These are just a few of the many steps on a very long list. Some issues I have hardly mentioned, and I have not been able to go into much detail on others, but evidence and detailed policy proposals exist in abundance. In contrast with aid, where the evidence is at best ambiguous, taking action on these issues will have overwhelmingly positive consequences for Africa both in the short and long term. Taken as a whole these issues put aid into the shade. But action on them is proceeding at a snail's pace because decision-makers are not feeling enough political pressure to do anything. In fact, worse, they are feeling pressure, but this is coming from vested interests (farming lobbies, drugs firms, banks, oil companies) that stand to lose out if decisions to really benefit Africa are taken. When was the last time thousands of people gathered in Trafalgar Square or at the Lincoln Memorial to demand more policy freedom for African governments, or a clamp down on tax havens?

People concerned about Africa need to think hard how they are going to spend their time, money and energy. We are all only human, and we are all busy people. We cannot do everything. If we spend the weekend writing letters calling for more aid we might not have time to delve into how to halt the brain drain. In order to free up time and space to put pressure where it really counts something will have to give. I think we should drop calling for more aid from our list of priorities. Even if you cannot agree that aid is doing harm, the evidence suggests that there are more important things we should be focusing on. Regarding aid itself, we should focus exclusively on improving its impacts, rather than calling for more. And we should ratchet up the pressure on the range of other issues that could really make a difference to the poor and marginalized in Africa.

Rich countries cannot claim to be pro-development while simultaneously failing to act to stem the illegal leaks from Africa which are going through tax havens under their control or influence. You cannot be pro-Africa if you are forcing African countries to sign up to rules on international property rights that manifestly harm their interests. If you are failing to act on climate change. If you insist on African countries reducing protection while continuing to protect your own industries. If you continue to collect on odious debts contracted by vicious dictators, while not returning stolen money. If you are benefiting from the brain drain without doing what you can to stop it. If you are failing to regulate businesses acting overseas. If you are making money from an arms trade that is causing turmoil in much of Africa. If you are propping up failing and corrupt regimes for short-term strategic gain.

Western politicians are failing to take the actions necessary to stop these and other manifest injustices. They come out of summit meetings offering the sop of more aid to Africa – but aid is not the answer. Rather than calling for more we should be sending our politicians back into their meeting rooms until they emerge with something that works.

Notes

1 *Time to think again*

1 OECD figures for 2007. Available at www.oecd.org.

2 See www.onevote08.org/ontherecord/.

3 This saying, popularly attributed to Bob Geldof, which he never actually said, is an amalgamation of two things he did say during the first Live Aid concert in 1985: 'People are dying now. Give us the money now' and 'Fuck the address, just give the phone, here's the number ...'

4 'We must do better', Trends in Development Assistance, remarks by Angel Gurria, OECD Secretary-General, Tokyo, 4 April 2008, www.oecd.org/document/7/0,3343,es_2649_201185_40385351_1_1_1_1,00.html.

5 OECD data and World Development Indicators online.

6 Isooba 2005.

7 Lwanga-Ntale 2005.

8 Kamara 2005.

9 Oxfam International on the G8 outcome, www.oxfam.ca/news-and-publications/news/oxfam-international-on-the-g8-outcome/view.

10 Speech by the Rt Hon. Gordon Brown MP, Chancellor of the Exchequer, at the Commission for Africa Meeting, Cape Town, South Africa, 17 January 2005, 213.225.140.43/English/about/pressroom/speeches/17-01-05_ev_speech_brown_cape_town.pdf.

11 It is probably worth acknowledging that in some international relations circles the term 'realism' has quite hawkish, *realpolitik*, connotations. It is not intended to have such connotations in this context.

12 Eddie Barnes, 30 December 2007, 'Africa needs more than a Band Aid after 23 years of failure', news.scotsman.com/opinion/Africa-needs-more-than-a.3628231.jp.

2 *The new aid era*

1 In 1960 seventeen African countries gained their independence, with one or two gaining independence per year over the following decade.

2 Weisbrot, Baker and Rosnick 2005.

3 Rodrik 1998.

4 World Development Indicators.

5 OECD data available at www.oecd.org.

6 World Bank 2007a.

7 Ibid. Donor country aid is measured by the OECD as a percentage of gross national income (GNI) rather than gross domestic product (GDP). GNI is the value of

all goods and services produced in a country in one year (GDP), plus transfers of income from other countries, such as foreign investment inflows, repatriation of profits on foreign investment, remittances of migrants, minus transfers of income to other countries, such as outflows of foreign direct investment and profits on foreign direct investment, transfers of income by foreigners.

8 OECD data available at www.oecd.org.

9 Ibid.

10 World Bank 2007b .

11 Manning 2005.

12 OECD data available at www.oecd.org.

13 Bush 2002, OECD data available at www.oecd.org.

14 betteraid.org, 18 February 2008, Bush in Africa: insights on US aid, betteraid.org/blog/?p=71.

15 OECD data available at www.oecd.org.

16 Ibid.

17 2007 Pre-Budget Report and Comprehensive Spending Review statement to the House of Commons, delivered by the Rt Hon. Alistair Darling MP, Chancellor of the Exchequer, www.hm-treasury.gov.uk/pbr_csr/pbr_csr07_speech.cfm.

18 BBC website, 24 May 2005, Chancellor hails EU aid agreement, news.bbc.co.uk/2/hi/uk_news/politics/4576321.stm.

19 OECD data available at www.oecd.org.

20 Ibid.

21 Bank Information Center, 18 December 2007, 'Donors Promise $8.9 Billion to the African Development Bank', www.bicusa.org/en/Article.3633.aspx.

22 Davies 2007.

23 China.org.cn, 30 April 2007, China's Eight Steps for Aid to Africa, www.china.org.cn/english/features/adb/209799.htm.

24 Jamil Anderlini, 25 June 2007, China insists on 'tied aid' in Africa, www.ft.com/cms/s/908c24f2-2343-11dc-9e7e-000b5df10621.html.

25 The Hindu Business Line, 9 April 2008, 'Imports from 50 Poor Nations to be Duty-free', www.thehindubusinessline.com/2008/04/09/stories/2008040952410100.htm.

26 UN Millennium Project 2005.

27 Commission for Africa 2005.

28 World Bank, Africa Development Indicators.

29 United Nations 2002, paragraph 39.

30 World Bank 2007a.

31 Kebede 2007.

32 United Nations 2005, p. 66.

33 See Easterly 2002 for an excellent summary.

34 World Development Indicators.

35 Not including South Africa and Nigeria. Data from World Development Indicators.

36 World Development Indicators.

37 Rodrik 1998.

38 Pearson 1969.

39 World Bank 2007a.

3 *All aid's impacts*

1 World Health Organization 1999.

2 Levine 2007, which includes a helpful discussion of successful public health interventions using aid money and foreign expertise.

3 Oxfam International 2005.

4 According to the Measles Initiative, www.measlesinitiative.org.

5 African Union 2005.

6 Global Campaign for Education 2005.

7 Oxfam 2005.

8 Ibid.

9 Ibid.

10 People's Health Movement, 9 April 2006, 'Zambia scraps healthcare fees for poor rural people', www.phmovement.org/cms/en/node/153.

11 Jubilee USA 2005.

12 Calderisi 2006.

13 Oxfam International 2005.

14 Riddell 2007.

15 World Bank 1999.

16 Eurodad 2008a, p. 14.

17 Christian Aid 2006.

18 Calderisi 2006.

19 Ibid.

20 Ibid., p. 190.

21 Ibid.

22 Lisa Margonelli, *New York Times*, 12 February 2007, 'The Short, Sad History of Chad's "Model" Oil Project', pipeline.blogs.nytimes.com/2007/02/12/the-short-sad-history-of-chads-model-oil-project/ and Bretton Woods Project, 20 January 2006, 'Bank freezes pipeline funds to Chad', www.brettonwoodsproject.org/art-507557.

23 Amnesty International 2005.

24 *Guardian*, 17 January 2007, 'Trouble in the pipeline', www.guardian.co.uk/environment/2007/jan/17/energy.society.

25 See www.bicusa.org/en/Project.24.aspx.

26 See www.internationalrivers.org/en/africa for more information on these projects.

27 Davies 2007.

4 *Pulling the strings*

1 IMF 2002.

2 See Williamson 2004 for an overview of the 'Washington Consensus'.

3 Stiglitz 2004.

4 Chang 2002.

5 Christian Aid 2004.

6 Oxfam 2002.

7 Christian Aid 2004.

8 Ibid.

9 UNCTAD 2007.

10 Baunsgaard and Keen 2005.

11 SCIAF Christian Aid and ACTSA 2007.

12 Ibid., p. 6.

13 Leach 2002.

14 Fraser and Lungu 2007.

15 Ibid.

16 Ibid.

17 Ibid.

18 Christian Aid 2006.

19 Ibid., p. 25.

20 Ibid.

21 Ibid.

22 Colclough and Lewin 1993.

23 Oxfam International 2003.

24 Global Campaign for Education 2006.

25 Christian Aid 2006.

26 UNCTAD 2007.

27 World Bank and IMF 2004.
28 IMF 1998.
29 Newbrander and Johnston 1998.
30 Simms, Rowson and Peattie 2001.
31 Mwanza 1998.
32 Kasese 1995.
33 Mwanza 1998 and Ahrin-Tenkorang 2000.
34 DfID 2002.
35 UNICEF 1998.
36 Bennett and Gilson 2001, p. 11.
37 Collier 2000, p. 10.
38 UNCTAD 2007.
39 Christian Aid 2004, p. 1.
40 Agha and Driscoll 2006.
41 Burnside and Dollar 1997.
42 De Renzio and Hanlon 2007.
43 Bergamaschi 2007.
44 World Bank 2000a.
45 The PRSP approach was initially linked to debt relief for countries in the Highly Indebted Poor Countries (HIPC) initiative but then expanded to cover other recipient countries as well.
46 Oxfam 2005.
47 Oxfam 2004.
48 IMF 2003.
49 Alexander 2007.
50 Eurodad 2008a.
51 Chair's Summary, Gleneagles Summit, 8 July 2005, see www.g8.gov.uk/servlet/Front?pagename=OpenMarket/Xcelerate/ShowPage&c=Page&cid=1119518698846.
52 IMF 1979.
53 IMF 2008.
54 Christian Aid 2006. This list includes binding and non-binding conditions.
55 Eurodad 2007b.
56 Christian Aid 2006.
57 Ibid.
58 Ibid.
59 Oxfam 2005.
60 Christian Aid 2006.
61 World Bank 2005a.
62 OECD 2006b.
63 Christian Aid 2008.
64 Eurodad 2008b.
65 Christian Aid 2008.
66 World Bank official aide-memoir to Ghana's Attorney General, 2003, cited in Christian Aid 2008, p. 15.
67 Christian Aid 2008, p. 7.
68 Ibid.
69 Barkan 2004.
70 UNCTAD 2007.
71 De Renzio and Hanlon 2007.
72 Agencia de Informacao de Mocambique, 'Donors imposed policies on Mozambique, Chissano admits', 12 June 2007, allafrica.com/stories/200706120859.html.
73 Ibid.
74 Speech to a World Bank public hearing in The Hague, quoted in a personal note sent to the author.
75 Christian Aid 2005.
76 Structural Adjustment Participatory Review Initiative 2004.
77 Oxfam 2006.

5 *Institutions, institutions, institutions*

1 Christian Aid 2005, p. 31.
2 *The Statesman*, 1 February

2008, 'The dying state of Ghana's poultry', www.thestatesman online.com/pages/news_detail.php?newsid=5675§ion=2.

3 Breisinger et al. 2008.

4 Ibid.

5 Dowden 2004.

6 Commission for Africa 2005, p. 14.

7 Ibid.

8 World Bank 1994.

9 Brian Levy and Sahr Kpundeh (eds) (2005), *State Capacity in Africa: New Approaches, Emerging Lessons* (Washington, DC: World Bank Institute) and OED (2005) *Capacity Building in Africa: An OED Evaluation of Bank Support* (Washington, DC: World Bank), cited in Moss et al. 2006.

10 Eurodad 2008a, p. 43.

11 World Bank 2005a.

12 Wood 2005.

13 OECD statistics cited in Fritz and Rocha Menocal 2007, p. 544.

14 Wamugo and Skadkær Pedersen 2007.

15 Cooksey 2004.

16 Hayman 2007, p. 20.

17 This section on Zambia relies on Fraser and Lungu 2007.

18 'IMF debt relief plan fails Uganda', 13 December 2002, www.news.bbc.co.uk/2/hi/business/2572337.stm.

19 'Zambia to re-think privatisation', 11 February 2003 www.news.bbc.co.uk/2/hi/business/2749219.stm.

20 Helleiner et al. 1995.

21 Harrison and Mulley 2007, p. 5.

22 *Guardian*, 25 May 2005, 'Flagship water privatisation fails in Tanzania', www.guardian.co.uk/politics/2005/may/25/uk.world.

23 Harrison and Mulley 2007.

24 Killick 2004b and Campos and Pradhan 1996 respectively.

25 Bergamaschi 2007, p. 7.

26 De Renzio and Hanlon 2007.

27 Eurodad 2008b.

28 De Renzio and Hanlon 2007.

29 Marcus and Wilkinson 2002. This study analysed six full and seventeen interim PRSPs.

30 Bergamaschi 2007, p. 2.

31 Mamane Sani Adamou of the Nigerian civil society organization Alternative Espaces Citoyens, quoted in Eurodad 2008a, p. 18.

32 Lockwood 2005.

33 World Bank 2003.

34 Fraser and Lungu 2007, p. 19.

35 Ibid.

36 *The Post*, July 18 2004, cited in Fraser and Lungu 2007.

37 Collier 1997.

38 As Bill Easterly points out on Dani Rodrik's blog, www.rodrik.typepad.com/dani_rodriks_weblog/2007/07/easterly-takes-.html.

39 Eurodad 2008a.

40 Ibid.

41 Eurodad 2008b, p. 11.

42 World Bank 2007a.

43 Eurodad 2008a.

44 Ibid.

45 Bergamaschi 2007, p. 6.

46 ESSD-Banque Mondiale/CEPIA – Mali (2006). 'Les implications structurelles de la libéralisation sur l'agriculture et le développement rural au Mali', cited in Bergamaschi 2007.

47 World Bank 1996.

48 ODI 2006.

49 Fraser and Lungu 2007.

50 Eurodad 2008a, p. 43.

51 Furtado and Smith 2007.

52 Knack 2000.

53 Personal communication to the author.

54 Eurodad 2008b.

55 Eurodad 2008a.

56 Ibid.

57 UNCTAD 2006.

58 UNCTAD 2007, p. 34.

59 World Bank 2007a.

60 Oxfam 2005, p. 54.

61 Transparency International 2007.

62 *Guardian*, 13 February 2003, 'An assault on poverty is vital too', www.www.guardian.co.uk/politics/2003/feb/13/foreignpolicy.famine.

63 Hanlon 2004.

64 *Guardian*, 14 January 2007, 'War zone aid "fuels more conflicts"', www.guardian.co.uk/society/2007/jan/14/internationalaidanddevelopment.internationalnews.

65 Alesina and Weder 2002.

66 Sachs 2005, for example, argues that if aid succeeds in raising civil service and other salaries, there will be fewer incentives to resort to corruption.

67 Moss et al. 2006, p. 15.

68 *The Times*, 24 March 2008, 'How the UN is feeding tyranny in Robert Mugabe's Zimbabwe', www.timesonline.co.uk/tol/comment/columnists/guest_contributors/article3607506.ece.

69 Virginie Baudais (2006), 'L'institutionalisation de l'Etat en Afrique: Les trajectoires comparées du Mali et du Niger' (Université de Toulouse: PhD thesis), quoted in Bergamaschi 2007.

70 Knack 2000.

71 Ibid., p. 4.

72 World Bank 2005b.

73 Gupta et al. 2005.

74 UNECA (2005), *Economic Report on Africa 2005: Meeting the Challenges of Unemployment and Poverty in Africa* (Addis Ababa: UNECA), cited in UNCTAD 2007.

75 Commission for Africa 2005 and Fagernas and Roberts 2004.

76 Gupta et al. 2004.

77 Sen Gupta 2007.

78 Manning 2006.

79 Chossudovsky 1997.

80 Kanbur 2000, p. 2.

6 Aid and growth

1 *Guardian*, 13 February 2003, 'An assault on poverty is vital too', www.guardian.co.uk/politics/2003/feb/13/foreignpolicy.famine. Gordon Brown was Chancellor of the Exchequer at the time.

2 Treichel 2005.

3 Chen and Ravallion (2007). 'Absolute Poverty Measures for the Developing World, 1981–2004', World Bank Working Paper No. 4211, Development Research Group (Washington, DC: World Bank), cited in UNCTAD 2007.

4 Treichel 2005.

5 UNCTAD 2007, p. 3.

6 Ibid.

7 Ibid.

8 World Bank 2006, p. xiii.

9 Woodward 2007b.

10 Woodward and Simms 2006.

11 Clemens et al. 2004.

12 Notably by Peter Boone, whose views are summarized in Alesina and Dollar 2000.

13 Jepma 1997.

14 Burnside and Dollar 1997. In 2004 Burnside and Dollar produced another paper arguing that in the 1990s aid to low income countries did go to countries with better policies, showing that selectivity was improving.

15 Clemens et al. 2004.

16 Rajan and Subramanian 2005, pp. 1 and 5.

17 Roodman 2004, cover page.

18 Easterly 2003, p. 35.

19 Foster and Killick 2006.

20 Dutch Disease is so called because it was first noted as a problem in Holland in the 1970s where the manufacturing sector suffered a decline after the exploitation of North Sea gas began in earnest. Originally coined with specific reference to the exploitation of natural resources it now refers to any boom in foreign earnings.

21 Bourguignon and Sundberg 2006, p. 6.

22 IMF (2005), *Monetary and Fiscal Policy Design Issues in Low Income Countries* (Washington, DC: IMF), cited in Gupta, Powell and Yang 2005.

23 Rajan and Subramanian 2005.

24 Gupta et al. 2005.

25 Following early work by Bauer 1972.

26 Birdsall 2007.

27 Jones Zulu 2006.

28 See for example Rajan and Subramanian 2005.

29 See for example Bourguignon and Leipziger 2006.

7 *A better future?*

1 OECD 2005. This list uses some notes from Eurodad 2008a to explain the concepts.

2 ActionAid 2005.

3 Eurodad 2008a.

4 Eurodad 2007a.

5 Alexander 2007.

6 Manning 2004.

7 Eurodad 2008a, p. 37.

8 UNDP 2006.

9 World Bank 2007a and Roodman 2006.

10 ActionAid 2006.

11 Reality of Aid 2007, p. 19.

12 See betteraid.org, 2008, p. 6.

13 Alexander 2007.

14 Eurodad 2008b.

15 Eurodad 2008a, p. 20.

16 Ibid.

17 ODI 2007.

18 Killick 2004a.

19 Euordad 2008a, p. 20 (emphasis added).

20 DfID 2005, p. 2.

21 Quoted in Easterly 2003, p. 25.

22 See the MCA website, at www.mcc.gov/selection/indicators/index.php.

23 Christian Aid 2006.

24 Bourguignon and Sundberg 2006, p. 2, and Bourguignon and Leipziger 2006, p. 8.

25 *Guardian*, 13 February 2003, 'An assault on poverty is vital too', www.guardian.co.uk/politics/2003/feb/13/foreignpolicy.famine.

26 See betteraid.org, 2008, p. 4.

27 De Long and Eichengreen 1991.

28 World Development Indicators.

29 World Development Indicators. Average since 2000, excluding Nigeria and South Africa.

30 Moss and Subramanian 2005.

8 *Why is aid really going up?*

1 Rajan and Subramanian 2005, p. 5.

2 Ibid., p. 20.

3 Dollar 2007, Deaton and Kozel 2005.

4 Oxfam 2005.

5 See for example Birdsall et al. 2005.

6 Quoted in Hancock 1992, p. 71.

7 Burnside and Dollar 1997.

8 USAID Greenbook, qesdb.cdie.org/gbk/index.html.

9 Woodward 2007a.

10 USAID Greenbook, qesdb.cdie.org/gbk/index.html.

11 AllAfrica.com, 23 February 2003, Washington Lobbies for Africa's UN Council Votes, allafrica.com/stories/200302260001.html.

12 Figures from USAID Greenbook, qesdb.cdie.org/gbk/index.html.

13 Dreher et al. 2006.

14 *Guardian*, 17 December 2006, 'US accused of using aid to sway votes in UN security council', www.guardian.co.uk/world/2006/dec/17/usa.internationalaidanddevelopment.

15 'Indeed, it is not merely right, but is in our long-term interest to offer a helping hand out of poverty to the poorest regions of the world', Tony Blair, House of Commons, 7 March 2001, cited in Barder 2005, p. 3.

16 Barder 2005.

17 Natsios 2006, pp. 131–2.

18 Christian Science Monitor, 11 April 2008, 'US military expands role in West Africa'.

19 US government website, 6 February 2007, 'U.S. Creating New Africa Command to Coordinate Military Efforts', www.america.gov/st/washfile-english/2007/February/20070206 170933M VyelwarCo.2182581.html.

20 Hansard, 20 February 1980 Cols 464–5. Cited in Barder 2005, p. 9.

21 *Financial Times*, 5 September 2006, 'China intervenes in Zambian election', www.ft.com/cms/s/0/d6d5d176-3d0a-11db-8239-0000779e2340.html?nclick_check=1 .

22 BBC, 3 January 2008, 'China ships food aid to Zimbabwe', news.bbc.co.uk/2/hi/africa/7170374.stm.

23 The Hindu Business Line, 9 April 2008, 'Imports from 50 poor nations to be duty-free', www.thehindubusinessline.com/2008/04/09/stories/2008040952410100.htm.

24 OECD 2006a.

25 Eurodad 2006 and actionaiditaly.blogspot.com, 15 May 2008, NGO resources contributing to Italian tied aid.

26 Betteraid.org, 13 November 2007, 'Italian businesses continues to benefit from tied aid', betteraid.org/blog/?p=53.

27 Care International, 'CARE turns down US food aid', www.careinternational.org.uk/CARE%20turns%20down%20US%20food%20aid+9831.twl.

28 BBCwebsite, 29 October 2002, 'Famine-hit Zambia rejects GM food aid', news.bbc.co.uk/2/hi/africa/2371675.stm.

29 Christian Aid 2008, p. 4.

30 *Sunday Times*, 9 March 2008, 'Sir Bob Geldof's travels with George Bush', www.timesonline.co.uk/tol/news/world/africa/article3510768.ece.

31 What is IMF? Cristina Kirchner's National TV Campaign for the 2007 elections, youtube.com/watch?v=lmDzlUvIM8A.

32 BBC website, 14 December 2005, 'Brazil to pay off IMF debts early', news.bbc.co.uk/2/hi/business/4527438.stm.

33 *India Daily*, 2 January 2005, 'India in its transition from the nation in need of a handout to an emerging superpower ready to flex its financial strength', www.indiadaily.com/editorial/01-02c-05.asp.

34 Oxfam 2007b.

35 Zambia HIPC paper.

36 Save the Children UK accounts available at www.savethechildren.org.uk/en/54_3249.htm.

37 Care USA accounts available at www.care.org/newsroom/publications/annualreports/index.asp.

38 ActionAid 2005 and 2006.

9 *What is to be done?*

1 The UK government never accepts this explicitly, but it is a concern of many other donors, see for instance EC 2005.

2 Oxfam 2007b.

3 Boyce and Ndikumana 2008.

4 World Development Indicators online.

5 Salisu 2005.

6 ActionAid 2005.

7 Boyce and Ndikumana 2003 and 2008.

8 Baker 2005.

9 Pak 2006.

10 Baker 2005.

11 Africa APPG 2006. It is not clear how corruption is defined in this calculation – it seems like a very high figure.

12 Chang 2007.

13 Raymond Baker, Center for International Policy, Washington, in oral evidence to the UK All Party Parliamentary Group on Africa in January 2006.

14 Rodrik 2001, p. 16.

15 David Murray, Transparency International UK, in oral evidence to the UK All Party Parliamentary Group on Africa in December 2005.

16 Transparency International 2004.

17 Human Rights Watch website, Nigerian Government Efforts to Fight Corruption, www.hrw.org/reports/2007/nigeria0107/9.htm#_ftn349.

18 Christian Aid website, 'Corruption: facts and figures', www.

christianaid.org.uk/stoppoverty/powercorruption/facts/index.aspx.

19 Christensen and Guindja 2005.

20 Publish What You Pay and Revenue Watch Institute 2006.

21 Africa APPG 2006.

22 Stiglitz 2006.

23 Weaver et al. 2003.

24 UNCTAD 2004.

25 Oxfam 2007b.

26 See www.odiousdebts.org.

27 Address by Trevor Manuel MP to the Fourth Meeting of the Forum on Tax Administration, 10 January 2008, Cape Town, www.treasury.gov.za/comm_media/speeches/2008/2008011001.pdf.

28 African Development Indicators.

29 UNCTAD 2007.

30 Ibid., p. 42.

31 Ibid.

32 Ibid.

33 *Guardian*, 31 October 2007, 'This is not a poker game', www.guardian.co.uk/comment/story/0,,2201993,00.html.

34 'We have said throughout, and I say again now, this can never be done on the basis of the old relationship of charity between donor and recipient, it can only be done on the basis of a partnership', Presidency Press Conference at Gleneagles, 8 July 2005.

35 Chang 2007.

36 Ibid.

37 However, patent reform would still be necessary, as without it the cost of publicly funded medical (or other technological) research would be unnecessarily inflated.

38 *The Independent*, 6 November 2006, 'Africa will be worst hit by climate change', www.independent.co.uk/environment/climate-change/africa-will-be-worst-hit-by-climate-change-423143.html.

39 UNDP 2005.

40 See, for example, Hagopian et al. 2005.

41 Jones Zulu 2006 and Eurodad 2008a.

42 Oxfam 2007a.

Bibliography

All websites last accessed on 29 May 2008 unless otherwise stated.

ActionAid (2005). *Real Aid: An Agenda for Making Aid Work* (London: ActionAid International).

— (2006). *Real Aid 2: Making Technical Assistance Work* (London: ActionAid International).

ActionAid International USA (2005). *Changing Course: Alternative Approaches to Achieve the Millennium Development Goals and Fight HIV/AIDS* (Washington, DC: ActionAid International USA).

Africa APPG (2006). 'The Other Side of the Coin: The UK and Corruption in Africa, Report of the Africa All Party Parliamentary Group', www.africaappg.org.uk.

African Union (2005). Observations and Recommendations of the First AU Conference of African Ministers of Economy and Finance (CAMEF), 7 May 2005, Dakar, Senegal, www.africa-union.org/root/UA/Conferences/novembre/EA/20-23%20nov/Exchange%20Of%20Views%20On%20Some%20Topical%20Economic%20Issues%20Rev%2011.pdf.

Afrodad (2007). *Aid Effectiveness in Africa: A Synthesis* (Harare: Afrodad).

Agha, Zainab Kizilbash and Ruth Driscoll (2006). Literature Review on Growth and Trade in Poverty Reduction Strategies, Overseas Development Institute, www.odi.org.uk/IEDG/Projects/Aid4trade_files/Growth_and_Trade_in_PRSs_Final_Report_Annex_A.pdf.

Alesina, Alberto and Beatrice Weder (2002). 'Do Corrupt Governments Receive Less Foreign Aid?', *American Economic Review* 92(4): 1126–37.

— and David Dollar (2000). 'Who Gives Foreign Aid to Whom and Why?', *Journal of Economic Growth*, 5(1): 33–63.

Alexander, Nancy (2007). 'The New Aid Model: Implications for the Aid System, Citizen's Network on Essential Services', unpublished paper.

Amnesty International (2005). *Contracting out of Human Rights: The Chad–Cameroon Pipeline Project* (London: Amnesty International UK).

Arhin-Tenkorang, D. (2000). 'Mobilizing Resources for Health: The Case for User Fees Revisited, Commission on Macroeconomics and Health',

Working Paper Series, Paper No. WG3:6 (Geneva).
Baker, Raymond (2005). *Capitalism's Achilles Heel: Dirty Money and How to Renew the Free-Market System* (New Jersey: John Wiley).
Barder, Owen (2005). 'Reforming Development Assistance: Lessons from the UK Experience', Center for Global Development Working Paper No. 70 (Washington, DC: Center for Global Development).
Barkan, Joel D. (2004). 'Kenya After Moi', *Foreign Affairs*, January/February.
Bauer, Peter (1972) *Dissent on Development* (Cambridge, MA: Harvard University Press).
Baunsgaard, Thomas and Michael Keen (2005). 'Tax Revenue and (or?) Trade Liberalization' (Washington, DC: International Monetary Fund), www.imf.org/external/pubs/ft/wp/2005/wp05112.pdf.
Bennett S. and Gilson L. (2001). *Health Financing: Designing and Implementing Pro-Poor Policies* (London: Department for International Development).
Bergamaschi, Isaline (2007). 'Mali: Patterns and Limits of Donor-driven Ownership, Managing Aid Dependency Project', Global Economic Governance Programme Working Paper No. 2007/31 (University College, Oxford), www.globaleconomicgovernance.org/.
Birdsall, Nancy (2007) 'Do No Harm: Aid, Weak Institutions and the Missing Middle in Africa', *Development Policy Review*, 25(5): 575–98.
— Dani Rodrik and Arvind Subramanian (2005). 'If Rich Governments Really Cared About Development', *Foreign Affairs*, July/August.
Bourguignon, François and Danny Leipziger (2006). *Aid, Growth and Poverty Reduction* (Washington, DC: World Bank).
— and Mark Sundberg (2006). 'Constraints to Achieving the MDGs with Scaled-Up Aid', DESA Working Paper No. 15 (Washington, DC: World Bank).
Boyce, James K. and Léonce Ndikumana (2003). 'Public Debts and Private Assets: Explaining Capital Flight from Sub-Saharan African Countries', *World Development*, 31(1): 107–30.
— (2008). 'Capital Flight from Sub-Saharan Africa', *Tax Justice Focus*, 4(1): 5–6.
Breisinger, Clemens, Xinshen Diao, James Thurlow, Bingxin Yu and Shashidhara Kolavalli (2008). 'Accelerating Growth and Structural Transformation: Ghana's Options for Reaching Middle-Income Country Status', IFPRI Discussion Paper 00750, International Food Policy Research Institute.
Burnside, Craig and David Dollar (1997). 'Aid, Policies and Growth', World Bank, Policy Research Working Paper No. 1777, www.worldbank.org/aid/background/toc.htm (Washington, DC: World Bank).

— (2004). 'Aid, Policies, and Growth: Revisiting the Evidence', World Bank Policy Research Working Paper No. 3251 (Washington, DC: World Bank).

Bush, George W. (2002). Speech at the United Nations Financing for Development Conference in Monterrey, Mexico, www.pbs.org/newshour/updates/march02/bush_3-22.html.

Calderisi, Robert (2006). *The Trouble with Africa: Why Foreign Aid isn't Working* (New Haven, CT: Yale University Press).

Campos, Edward and Sanjay Pradhan (1996). 'Budgetary Institutions and Expenditure Outcomes: Binding Governments to Fiscal Performance', World Bank Policy Research Working Paper No.1646 (Washington, DC: World Bank).

Chang, Ha-Joon (2002). *Kicking Away the Ladder: Policies and Institutions for Economic Development in Historical Perspective* (London: Anthem Press).

— (2007). *Bad Samaritans: Rich Nations, Poor Policies and the Threat to the Developing World* (London: Random House).

Chossudovsky, Michael (1997). *The Globalization of Poverty. Impacts of IMF and World Bank Reforms* (London: Zed Books).

Christensen, John and Pierre Guindja (2005). 'The Africa Question: Where Do All the Profits Go?', *Tax Justice Focus*, 1(1): 1–2.

Christian Aid (2003). *Struggling To Be Heard: Democratising the World Bank and IMF* (London: Christian Aid).

— (2004). *Taking Liberties: Poor People, Free Trade and Trade Justice* (London: Christian Aid).

— (2005). *The Damage Done: Aid, Death and Dogma* (London: Christian Aid).

— (2006). *Challenging Conditions: A New Strategy for Reform at the World Bank and IMF* (London: Christian Aid).

— (2008). *Buying Power: Aid, Governance and Public Procurement* (London: Christian Aid).

Clemens, Michael, Steven Radelet and Rikhil Bhavnani (2004). 'Counting Chickens When They Hatch: The Short Term Effect of Aid on Growth', Center for Global Development Working Paper No. 44 (Washington, DC: Center for Global Development).

Colclough C. and Lewin K. (1993) *Educating All the Children* (Oxford: Clarendon Press).

Collier, P. (1997) 'The Failure of Conditionality', in C. Gwin and J. M. Nelson (eds), *Perspectives on Development* (Baltimore, MD: Johns Hopkins University Press).

— (2000) *Consensus-building, Knowledge and Conditionality* (Washington, DC: World Bank).

Commission for Africa (2005). 'Our Common Interest: Report of the Commission for Africa', www.commissionforafrica.org/, accessed 21 April 2008.

Commission on Macroeconomics and Health (2001). 'Macroeconomics and Health: Investing in Health for Economic Development' (Geneva: World Health Organization).

Cooksey (2004). 'Elixir or Poison Chalice? The Relevance of Aid to East Africa', Paper prepared for the DAC Development Partnership Forum: Improving Donor Effectiveness in Combating Corruption organized jointly by OECD Development Assistance Committee and Transparency International, 9–10 December, www.oecd.org/dataoecd/42/11/34098651.PDF.

Davies, Penny (2007). 'China and the End of Poverty in Africa: Towards Mutual Benefit?', (Stockholm: Diakonia), see www.diakonia.se/sa/node.asp?node=2009.

De Long, J. Bradford and Barry Eichengreen (1991). 'The Marshall Plan: History's Most Successful Structural Adjustment Program', National Bureau of Economic Research Working Paper No. 3899 (Cambridge, MA: NBER).

De Renzio, Paolo and Joseph Hanlon (2007). 'Contested Sovereignty in Mozambique: The Dilemmas of Aid Dependence', Managing Aid Dependency Project, Global Economic Governance Programme Working Paper No. 2007, www.globaleconomicgovernance.org/25 (University College, Oxford).

Deaton, Angus and Valerie Kozel (2005). 'Data and Dogma: The Great Indian Poverty Debate', *World Bank Research Observer* 20: 177–99.

DfID (Department for International Development) (2002). *Reaching the Poor: The Costs of Sending Children to School* (London: DfID).

— (2005). *Partnerships for Poverty Reduction: Rethinking Conditionality* (London: DfID).

Dollar, David (2007). 'Poverty, Inequality and Social Disparities during China's Economic Reform', World Bank Policy Research Working Paper No. 4253 (Washington, DC: World Bank).

Dowden, R. (2004). 'Do Not Try to Save Africa, Try to Understand It', NRC/Handelsblad; Opinie en Debat. Cited in Bram van Ojik (2006) 'A Lesson in Modesty: In Search of the Legitimacy of Dutch Development Cooperation', www.minbuza.nl/binaries/en-pdf/thema-s-en-dossiers/quality-and-effectiveness/5_a_lesson_in_modesty.pdf, p. 48.

Dreher, Axel, Peter Nunnenkamp and Rainer Thiele (2006). 'Does US Aid Buy UN General Assembly Votes? A Disaggregated Analysis', Kiel Working Papers, No. 1275 (Kiel: Kiel Institute for the World Economy).

Easterly, William (2002) 'The Cartel of Good Intentions: The Problem of Bureaucracy in Foreign Aid', Institute for International Economics

(Washington, DC: Center for Global Development).
— (2003). 'Can Foreign Aid Buy Growth?', *Journal of Economic Perspectives*, 17(3): 23–48.
— (2005). 'Reliving the '50s: the Big Push, Poverty Traps, and Takeoffs in Economic Development', Center for Global Development Working Paper No. 65 (Washington, DC: Center for Global Development).
— (2006). *The White Man's Burden: Why the West's Efforts to Aid the Rest Have Done So Much Ill and So Little Good* (New York: Penguin).
— Ross Levine and David Roodman (2003). 'New Data, New Doubts: Revisiting "Aid, Policies, and Growth"', Center for Global Development Working Paper No. 26 (Washington, DC: Center for Global Development).
ESSD-Banque Mondiale/CEPIA – Mali (2006). 'Les implications structurelles de la libéralisation sur l'agriculture et le développement rural au Mali', cited in Bergamaschi 2007.
Ellerman, David (2007). *Helping People Help Themselves* (Ann Arbor: University of Michigan Press).
Eurodad (2006). *EU Aid: Genuine Leadership or Misleading Figures?* (Brussels: Eurodad).
— (2007a). *Putting Donors under Surveillance? A Eurodad Briefing on the Aid Effectiveness Agenda* (Brussels: Eurodad).
— (2007b). *Untying the Knots: How the World Bank is Failing to Deliver Real Change on Conditionality* (Brussels: Eurodad).
— (2008a). *Turning the Tables: Aid and Accountability under the Paris Framework* (Brussels: Eurodad), www.eurodad.org/uploadedFiles/Whats_New/Reports/Turning_the_Tables.pdf.
— (2008b) *Old Habits Die Hard: Aid and Accountability in Sierra Leone* (Brussels: Eurodad).
European Commission (2005). 'New Sources of Financing for Development: A Review of Options', Commission of the European Communities Staff Working Paper, ec.europa.eu/taxation_customs/resources/documents/sec_2005_467_en.pdf.
Fagernas, S. and J. Roberts (2004). 'Fiscal Impact of Aid: A Survey of Issues and Synthesis of Country Studies of Malawi, Uganda and Zambia', ESAY Working Paper No. 11 (London: ODI).
Foster, Mick and Tony Killick (2006). 'What Would Doubling Aid Do for Macroeconomic Management in Africa?', Overseas Development Institute, Working Paper No. 264 (London: ODI).
Fraser, Alastair and John Lungu (2007). 'For Whom the Windfalls? Winners and Losers in the Privatisation of Zambia's Copper Mines', www.minewatchzambia.com/reports/report.pdf

Fritz, Verena and Alina Rocha Menocal (2007). 'Developmental States in the New Millennium: Concepts and Challenges for a New Aid Agenda', *Development Policy Review*, 25(5): 531–52.

Furtado, Xavier and W. James Smith (2007). 'Ethiopia: Aid, Ownership and Sovereignty, Managing Aid Dependency Project', Global Economic Governance Programme Working Paper 2007/28, www.globaleconomicgovernance.org/ (University College, Oxford).

Global Campaign for Education (2005). 'Missing the Mark: A School Report on Rich Countries' Contribution to Universal Primary Education by 2015'.

— (2006). 'Every Child Needs a Teacher, Campaign Brief, Global Campaign for Education', www.campaignforeducation.org.

Gunning, Jan Willem (2006). 'Aid Evaluation: Pursuing Development as if Evidence Matters', *Swedish Economic Policy Review*, 13: 145–63.

Gupta, Sanjeev, Benedict Clements, A. Pivovarsky and E. R. Tiongson (2004). 'Foreign Aid and Revenue Response: Does the Composition of Aid Matter?', in Sanjeev Gupta, Benedict Clements and Gabriela Inchauste (eds), *Helping Countries Develop: The Role of Fiscal Policy* (Washington, DC: IMF).

— Robert Powell and Yongzheng Yang (2005). 'The Macroeconomic Challenges of Scaling Up Aid to Africa', IMF Working Paper No. WP/05/179 (Washington, DC: IMF).

Hagopian, Amy, Anthony Ofosu, Adesegun Fatusi, Richard Biritwum, Ama Essel, L. Gary Hart and Carolyn Watts (2005). 'The Flight of Physicians from West Africa: Views of African Physicians and Implications for Policy', *Social Science & Medicine*, 61: 1750–60.

Hancock, Graham (1992). *Lords of Poverty: The Power, Prestige and Corruption of the International Aid Business* (New York: Atlantic Monthly Press).

Hanlon, Joseph (2004). 'Do Donors Promote Corruption? The Case of Mozambique', *Third World Quarterly*, 25(4): 747–63.

Harrison, Graham and Sarah Mulley (2007). 'Tanzania: A Genuine Case of Recipient Leadership in the Aid System?', Managing Aid Dependency Project, Global Economic Governance Programme Working Paper 2007/29, www.globaleconomicgovernance.org/ (University College, Oxford).

Hayman, Rachel (2007). 'Milking the Cow: Negotiating Ownership of Aid and Policy in Rwanda', Managing Aid Dependency Project, Global Economic Governance Programme Working Paper 2007/26, www.globaleconomicgovernance.org/ (University College, Oxford).

Helleiner, Gerald, Ndulu Lipumba and Svendsen (1995). Development Cooperation Issues Between Tanzania and Its Aid Donors: Report of the Group of Independent Advisers, Royal Danish Ministry of Foreign Affairs.

International Monetary Fund (IMF) (1979). *Guidelines on Conditionality* (Washington, DC: IMF).

— (1998). *External Evaluation of the ESAF*, Report by a Group of Independent Experts (Washington, DC: IMF).

— (2002). *Guidelines on Conditionality* (Washington, DC: IMF).

— (2003). *Evaluation of Poverty Reduction Strategy Papers and the Poverty Reduction and Growth Facility* (Washington, DC: IMF).

— (2008). 'The Gambia: Enhanced Heavily Indebted Poor Countries Initiative – Completion Point Document and Multilateral Debt Relief Initiative', IMF Country Report No. 08/109 (Washington, DC: IMF).

Isooba, Moses (2005). 'Southern Voices for Change in the International Aid Architecture: Listening and Learning from the Voices of the Civil Society. What Kind of Difference?', part of the Southern Voices Project of the Overseas Development Institute (London).

Jepma, C. (1997). *On the Effectiveness of Development Aid* (Washington, DC: World Bank).

Jones Zulu, Jack (2006). 'Zambia after the HIPC "surgery" and the Completion Point', Jesuit Centre for Theological Reflection, www.jctr.org.zm.

Jubilee USA (2005). 'First Step on a Long Journey: Putting the G-8 Deal on Debt into Perspective', www.jubileeusa.org/fileadmin/user_upload/Resources/Policy_Archive/First_Step_2005.pdf.

Kamara, Siapha (2005). 'Comments on Southern Voices for Change in the International Aid System Scoping Paper', part of the Southern Voices Project of the Overseas Development Institute (London).

Kanbur, Ravi (2000). 'Aid, Conditionality and Debt in Africa', revised version, in Finn Tarp (ed.), *Foreign Aid and Development: Lessons Learnt and Directions for the Future* (London: Routledge).

Kasese, E. (1995). 'Structural Adjustment and the Protection of the Poor: The Social Welfare Component of the "Social Development Fund" in Zimbabwe', in J. Balch, P. Johnson and R. Morgan, *Transcending the Legacy: Children in the New Southern Africa* (African European Institute/ SARDC, UNICEF), pp. 191–9.

Kebede, Behanu (2007). 'Partnerships for a Malaria-Free World', statement by Ethiopian Ambassador to the UK at the Africa Malaria Day event in the UK, www.coalitionagainstmalaria.org.uk/sites/uk-en/data/files/ambmalariacoalitionspeech.doc.

Killick, Tony (2004a). 'Politics, Evidence and the New Aid Agenda', *Development Policy Review*, 22(1): 29–53.

— (2004b). *The Democratic Deficit and the Politics of Ghana's Budgetary System* (Accra and London: Centre for Democratic Development and ODI).

Knack, Stephen (2000). 'Aid Dependence and the Quality of Governance: A Cross-Country Empirical Analysis', Policy Research Working Paper No. 2396 (Washington, DC: World Bank).

Leach, M. (2002). *Exploration of the Impact of Privatisation: Overview and Case Studies* (Oxford: Oxford Analytica).

Levine, Ruth (2007). 'Millions Saved: Proven Successes in Global Health' (Washington, DC: Centre for Global Development), www.cgdev.org/section/initiatives/_active/millionssaved/overview, accessed 21 April 2008.

Lockwood, Matthew (2005). *The State They're In: An Agenda for International Action on Poverty in Africa* (London: ITDG Publishing).

Lwanga-Ntale, Charles (2005). 'Comments on the Scoping Paper on Aid Architecture', part of the Southern Voices Project of the Overseas Development Institute, UK.

Manning, Richard (2004). 'How can the Development Community Help to Achieve Greater Progress towards the Millennium Development Goals?' (Helsinki: WIDER United Nations University).

— (2005). 'How Much New Aid is Really New Aid?', PowerPoint presentation, OECD, www.oecd.org/document/25/0,2340,en_2649_33721_35317145_1_1_1_1,00.html, accessed 21 April 2008.

— (2006). 'The "Big Picture" on Aid and the Paris Declaration', Presentation to the CAPE Conference (London: ODI, November).

Marcus, Rachel and John Wilkinson (2002). 'Whose Poverty Matters? Vulnerability, Social Protection and PRSPs', CHIP Working Paper No. 1 (London: Save the Children UK).

Moss, Todd and Arvind Subramanian (2005) 'After the Big Push? Fiscal and Institutional Implications of Large Aid Increases', Working Paper No. 71 (Washington, DC: Center for Global Development).

— Gunilla Pettersson and Nicolas van de Walle (2006). 'An Aid-Institutions Paradox? A Review Essay on Aid Dependency and State Building in Sub-Saharan Africa', Center for Global Development Working Paper No. 74 (Washington, DC: Center for Global Development).

Mwanza, A. (1998) *Effects of Economic Reform on Children and Youth in Zimbabwe* (Harare: Save the Children UK).

Natsios, Andrew S. (2006). 'Five Debates on International

Development: The US Perspective', *Development Policy Review*, 24(2): 131–9.

Newbrander W. and T. Johnston (1998). 'Protecting the Poor from the Impact of Increased User Charges in Government Health Facilities: What Works?', World Bank Health and Poverty Seminar Report (Washington, DC: World Bank).

ODI (Overseas Development Institute) (2006). 'Budget Support and Beyond: Can the Paris Agenda on Aid be Delivered?', CAPE Workshop Report, speech delivered by Jesse Griffiths of ActionAid UK 'Technical Assistance: Supporting or Undermining Accountability?' (London: ODI).

— (2007). 'Budget Support to Ghana: A Risk Worth Taking?', Briefing Paper 24 (London: ODI).

OECD (Organisation for Economic Co-operation and Development) (2005). *The Paris Declaration on Aid Effectiveness* (Paris: OECD).

— (2006a). *2005 Development Co-operation Report* (Paris: OECD).

— (2006b). 'Why is Procurement Important?', Factsheet, www.oecd/dac/effectiveness

Oxfam (2002). 'Cultivating Poverty: The Impact of US Cotton Subsidies on Africa', Oxfam Briefing Paper 30 (Oxford: Oxfam).

— (2003). *The IMF and the Millennium Goals: Failing to Deliver for Low Income Countries* (Oxford: Oxfam International).

— (2004). 'From "Donorship" to Ownership: Moving towards PRSP Round 2', Oxfam Briefing Paper 51 (Oxford: Oxfam).

— (2005). *Paying the Price: Why Rich Countries Must Invest Now in a War on Poverty* (Oxford: Oxfam International).

— (2006) 'Kicking the Habit: How the World Bank and the IMF are Still Addicted to Attaching Economic Policy Conditions to Aid', Oxfam Briefing Paper 96 (Oxford: Oxfam).

— (2007a). 'Africa's Missing Billions: International Arms Flows and the Cost of Conflict', Oxfam Briefing Paper 107 (Oxford: Oxfam).

— (2007b). 'The World is Still Waiting: Broken G8 Promises are Costing Millions of Lives', Oxfam Briefing Paper 103 (Oxford: Oxfam).

Pak, Simon J. (2006). 'Estimates of Capital Movements from African Countries to the United States through Trade Mispricing', paper given at tax research workshop at Essex University, UK, 7 July.

Pearson, Lester (1969). *Partners in Development: A Report of the Commission on International Development* (New York: Praeger).

Publish What You Pay and Revenue Watch Institute (2006). 'Eye on EITI: Civil Society Perspectives and Recommendations on the Extractive Industries Transparency Initiative' (London and New York).

Rajan, Raghuram G. and Arvind Subramanian (2005). 'Aid and Growth: What Does the Cross-Country Evidence Really Show?', IMF Working Paper No. WP/05/127 (Washington, DC: IMF).

Reality of Aid (2007). The Paris Declaration: Towards Enhanced Aid Effectiveness, Reality Check magazine, see www.ccic.ca/e/docs/002_aid_2007-01_reality_check_paris_dec.pdf.

Riddell, Roger (2007). *Does Foreign Aid Really Work?* (Oxford: Oxford University Press).

Rocha Menocal, Alina and Andrew Rogerson (2006). 'Which Way the Future of Aid? Southern Civil Society Perspectives on Current Debates on Reform to the International Aid System', ODI Working Paper No. 259 (London: ODI).

Rodrik, Dani (1998). 'Where Did All the Growth go? External Shocks, Social Conflict and Growth Collapses', ksghome.harvard.edu/~drodrik/conftext.pdf, accessed 21 April 2008.

— (2001). 'The Global Governance of Trade as if Development Really Mattered', report submitted to the United Nations Development Program (New York).

Roodman, David (2004). 'The Anarchy of Numbers: Aid, Development, and Cross-country Empirics', Center for Global Development Working Paper No. 32 (Washington, DC: Center for Global Development).

— (2006). 'Aid Project Proliferation and Absorptive Capacity', Center for Global Development Working Paper No. 75 (Washington, DC: Center for Global Development).

Sachs, Jeffrey (2005). *The End of Poverty: Economic Possibilities for Our Time* (New York: Penguin).

Salisu, Mohammed (2005). 'The Role of Capital Flight and Remittances in Current Account Sustainability in Sub-Saharan Africa', workshop in Accra, Ghana (UNECA).

SCIAF, Christian Aid and ACTSA (2007). 'Undermining development? Copper mining in Zambia', sciaf.live.visionwt.com/policy/undermining_development_copper_mining_in_zambia.

Sen Gupta, Abhijit (2007). 'Determinants of Tax Revenue Efforts in Developing Countries', IMF Working Paper No. 07/184 (Washington, DC: IMF).

Simms C., M. Rowson and S. Peattie (2001). *The Bitterest Pill of All: The Collapse of Africa's Health Systems* (London: Save the Children UK and MEDACT).

Stiglitz, Joseph (2004). 'The Post Washington Consensus Consensus, The Initiative for Policy Dialogue', wwwo.gsb.columbia.edu/ipd/pub/Stiglitz_PWCC_English1.pdf.

— (2006). *Making Globalization*

Work (New York: W. W. Norton).
Structural Adjustment Participatory Review Initiative (2004). *Structural Adjustment: The Policy Roots of Economic Crisis, Poverty and Inequality* (New York: Zed Books).
Transparency International (2004). *Global Corruption Report 2004*, www.transparency.org.
— (2007). 'Poverty, Aid and Corruption', TI Policy Paper No. 01/2007, www.transparency.org/publications/publications/aid_corruption.
Treichel, Volker (2005). 'Tanzania's Growth Process and Success in Reducing Poverty', IMF Working Paper No. WP/05/35 (Washington, DC: IMF).
UNCTAD (United Nations Conference on Trade and Development) (2004). *Economic Development in Africa: Debt Sustainability, Oasis or Mirage?* (New York: United Nations).
— (2006). *Economic Development in Africa: Doubling Aid: Making the 'Big Push' Work* (New York and Geneva: United Nations).
— (2007). *Economic Development in Africa: Reclaiming Policy Space: Domestic Resource Mobilization and Developmental States* (New York: United Nations).
UNDP (United Nations Development Programme) (2005). *Human Development Report 2005: International Cooperation at a Crossroads* (New York: United Nations).
— (2006). *The New Public Finance: Responding to Global Challenges* (New York: Oxford University Press).
UNICEF (1998). *State of the World's Children* (New York: UNICEF).
United Nations (2002). 'Monterrey Consensus on Financing for Development', New York, www.un.org/esa/ffd/, accessed 21 April 2008.
— (2005). 'Investing in Development: A Practical Plan to Achieve the Millennium Development Goals', New York, www.unmillenniumproject.org/, accessed 21 April 2008.
Wamugo, Erastus and Finn Skadkær Pedersen (2007). 'The Paris Agenda and Its Consequences for Civil Society in Kenya', Skadkaer Consult, www.skadkaer.dk/files/Paris-NGOsKenya.pdf.
Weaver, James, Randall Dodd and Jamie Baker (eds) (2003). 'Debating the Tobin Tax' (Washington, DC: New Rules for Global Finance Coalition).
Weisbrot, Mark, Dean Baker and David Rosnick (2005). 'The Scorecard on Development: 25 Years of Diminished Progress' (Washington, DC: Center for Economic and Policy Research).
Williamson, John (2004). 'A Short History of the Washington Consensus, Institute for International Economics', www.iie.com/publications/papers/williamson0904-2.pdf.
Wood, Angela (2005). *Demystifying*

'Good Governance': An Overview of World Bank Governance Reforms and Conditions (Dublin: Trocaire).

Woodward, David (2007a). 'Vote Buying in the UN Security Council', *The Lancet* (January) 369: 12–13.

— (2007b). 'Whistling in the Dark: Why the World Bank's Latest Poverty Projections are Meaningless', Jubilee Research at NEF (London: New Economics Foundation), www.jubileere search.org/news/Comment% 20on%20Global%20Ec%20Prospects%202007.pdf.

— and Andrew Simms (2006). 'Growth isn't Working: The Unbalanced Distribution of Benefits and Costs from Economic Growth' (London: New Economics Foundation).

World Bank (1994). *Governance: The World Bank's Experience, Development in Practice* (Washington, DC: World Bank).

— (1996). *Togo: Overcoming the Crisis, Population and Human Resources Operations Division* (Washington, DC: World Bank).

— (1999). *Annual Review of Development Effectiveness (ARDE): Toward a Comprehensive Development Strategy* (Washington, DC: World Bank).

— (2000a). *Assessing Aid: What Works, What Doesn't, and Why* (Washington, DC: World Bank).

— (2000b). *Attacking Poverty* (Oxford: Oxford University Press).

— (2003). *World Development Report 2004: Making Services Work For Poor People* (Washington, DC: World Bank).

— (2005a). *World Bank Review of Conditionality* (Washington, DC: World Bank).

— (2005b). *African Development Indicators 2005* (Washington, DC: World Bank)

— (2006). *Global Economic Prospects 2007: Managing the Next Wave of Globalization* (Washington, DC: World Bank).

— (2007a). *Aid Architecture: An Overview of the Main Trends in Official Development Assistance Flows* (Washington, DC: World Bank).

— (2007b) *Global Monitoring Report 2007* (Washington, DC: World Bank).

— and IMF (2004). PRSP Source Book, chapter 12, 'Macroeconomic Issues' (Washington DC: World Bank and IMF).

World Health Organization (1999). *World Health Organization Report on Infectious Diseases: Removing Obstacles to Healthy* Development (Geneva: World Health Organization).

www.betteraid.org (2008). 'Better Aid: A civil society position paper for the 2008 Accra High Level Forum on Aid Effectiveness', www.betteraid.org/downloads/Policy_Paper_printed_version.pdf.

Index